Bilingualism

PSYCHOLOGICAL, SOCIAL, AND EDUCATIONAL IMPLICATIONS

ACADEMIC PRESS RAPID MANUSCRIPT REPRODUCTION

Bilingualism
PSYCHOLOGICAL, SOCIAL, AND EDUCATIONAL IMPLICATIONS

edited by

Peter A. Hornby

Department of Psychology
State University of New York
Plattsburgh, New York

ACADEMIC PRESS, INC.   New York   San Francisco   London   1977
A Subsidiary of Harcourt Brace Jovanovich, Publishers

ACADEMIC PRESS, INC.
111 Fifth Avenue, New York, New York 10003

United Kingdom Edition published by
ACADEMIC PRESS, INC. (LONDON) LTD.
24/28 Oval Road, London NW1

Library of Congress Cataloging in Publication Data

Main entry under title:

Bilingualism.

    Proceedings of a Canadian–American conference on
bilingualism held March 12-13, 1976, on the Platts-
burgh Campus of the State University of New York.
    Includes index.
    1.   Bilingualism—Congresses.   I. Hornby,
Peter A.
P115.B55   301.2'1   77-1626
ISBN 0−12−356350−X

PRINTED IN THE UNITED STATES OF AMERICA

  81 82   9 8 7 6 5 4

Contents

List of Contributors

Numbers in parentheses indicate the pages on which authors' contributions begin.

SANDRA BEN-ZEEV (29), Bilingual Education Service Center, 500 South Dwyer Avenue, Arlington Heights, Illinois 60005

ROBERT L. COOPER (103), Department of Education, Hebrew University, Jerusalem, Israel

JOSHUA A. FISHMAN (103), Ferkauf Graduate School of Humanities and Social Sciences, Yeshiva University, 55 Fifth Avenue, New York, New York 10003

ELIZABETH GATBONTON (77), Department of Psychology, Concordia University, Sir George Williams Faculty of Arts, 1455 de Maisonneuve Blvd. West, Montreal, Quebec H3G 1M8

FRED GENESEE (147), Curriculum Department, The Protestant School Board of Greater Montreal, 6000 Fielding Avenue, Montreal, Quebec H3X 1T4

EINAR HAUGEN (91), Department of Germanic Languages and Literatures, Harvard University, Cambridge, Massachusetts 02138

PETER A. HORNBY (1), Department of Psychology, State University of New York, College of Arts and Science, Plattsburgh, New York 12901

WALLACE E. LAMBERT (15), Department of Psychology, McGill University, P.O. Box 6070, Station 'A', Montreal, Quebec H3C 3G1

P. D. McCORMACK (57), Department of Psychology, Carleton University, Ottawa, Canada K1S 5B6

YEHUDIT ROSENBAUM (103), Communications Program, Hebrew University, Jerusalem, Israel

NORMAN SEGALOWITZ (77), Department of Psychology, Concordia University, Sir George Williams Faculty of Arts, 1455 de Maisonneuve Blvd. West, Montreal, Quebec H3G 1M8

DONALD M. TAYLOR (67), Department of Psychology, McGill University, P.O. Box 6070, Station 'A', Montreal, Quebec H3C 3G1

G. RICHARD TUCKER (141), Department of Psychology, McGill University, P.O. Box 6070, Station 'A', Montreal, Quebec H3C 3G1

Preface

The present volume brings together some of the historical developments, theoretical controversies, and major research findings, as well as applications, from the disciplines of psychology, sociology, linguistics, and education as they relate to the diverse problems and benefits of bilingualism. Developments from each of these disciplines are brought to bear on the important question of what effect bilingualism may have on the individual language user and on the society in which he lives. The central focus of the volume is not, however, to judge whether bilingualism is in itself a beneficial or detrimental phenomenon. Rather, granting the fact that bilingualism is and will undoubtably continue to be a fact of life for the majority of the world's population, it was our goal to try to determine which characteristics of the bilingual setting lead to its being viewed as a source of enrichment and diversity, and hence to be encouraged, rather than as a source of confusion, conflict, and frustration.

Children throughout the world are educated in second and sometimes third languages, political and educational leaders must make and revise language policy decisions, and individuals often choose or are compelled to incorporate a second language into their repertoire. Although bilingualism has thus for many years been both a fact of life and an explosive political issue in many societies throughout the world, multidisciplinary efforts to study its effects systematically are quite new. Recently, however, changing social values as well as federal legislation in both the United States and Canada have led to an increased awareness of the need to better understand the implications of this complex phenomenon on the part of many components of our society.

Considerations of this type should be of interest to readers involved in the study of language from the disciplines of sociology, psychology, linguistics, and education, as well as the general reader whose interests include gaining a better understanding of major social and psychological influences. More specifically, persons interested in bilingual education and research, language planning and policy decisions, the structure and behavior of minority and immigrant populations, as well as the analysis of sociopolitical structures should find much of interest and value. It should be pointed out, however, that the present volume is in no sense intended to be a comprehensive treatment of bilingualism, even as it relates to these issues and interests. The contributors focus on those issues faced currently in their own research and thinking. These issues are among those at the forefront of contemporary considerations in the disciplines that they represent.

By bringing these interests from different disciplines together in one volume, it is possible for the reader to gain an awareness and appreciation of the scope and complexity of current thinking in bilingualism. Those wishing to explore further the many directions and avenues of current research in this area will find the references at the end of each chapter to be a valuable guide.

A depth of knowledge in the fields represented, while no doubt valuable, is not a prerequisite to benefiting from the present contributions. The authors have achieved a delicate balance between the theoretical and the applied aspects of their work, and the overall integration of the chapters is greatly enhanced by the final summary chapter as well as the introductory overview. It is hoped that the ideas presented in this volume will serve as a further stimulus to research and thinking and will lead also to increased interdisciplinary understanding of the complex issues involved.

This volume is the product of a Canadian–American conference devoted to the topic of bilingualism that was held on the Plattsburgh Campus of the State University of New York, March 12-13, 1976. The purpose of the conference was to bring together scholars from a variety of disciplines to discuss the problems and benefits associated with speaking more than one language. The conference was made possible through a grant from the James N. Rosenberg Fund and was cosponsored by the State University College at Plattsburgh.

Except for minor revisions and editorial changes, the individual contributions appear as they were originally presented at the conference. Unfortunately, Dr. McCormack was unable to be present at the conference; but his paper, included in the current volume, was presented and discussed by Dr. Genesee, who also agreed after the conference to prepare a summary and discussion of the proceedings to serve as the final chapter. The introductory chapter, although also not presented at the conference, was prepared by the editor and provides the necessary background for the individual contributions.

Acknowledgments

As coordinator of the conference and editor of this volume I would like to express my appreciation to the many people who assisted in the original planning and organization of the conference. In particular I wish to thank my colleagues, Roy Malpass and Philip DeVita for their encouragement and support. The cooperation and thoughtfulness of the individual contributors greatly simplified the task of organizing and coordinating the proceedings for publication, and I wish to express my appreciation for their help. I am particularly grateful for the pleasant and meticulous manner in which Joyce Armstrong worked on the preparation and typing of the final manuscript. In addition I would like to thank Academic Press for making the conference proceedings available to a wider audience. Finally, I wish to thank my wife Claudia, who, as always, provided enthusiastic support and assistance throughout the project.

Chapter 1

Bilingualism:
An Introduction and Overview

PETER A. HORNBY

State University of New York at Plattsburgh

For the average English-speaking American, the probability of being fluent in a second language is relatively remote.
Although many of us have elected or been required to study one
or more "foreign" languages, we have rarely attained nativelike fluency, and we would be unlikely to be considered or to
consider ourselves functionally bilingual. However, for a
large percentage of the peoples of the world, speaking more
than one language is a natural way of life with a variety of
factors determining which language will be spoken on any particular occasion (cf. Ervin-Tripp, 1964; Fishman, 1965). Most
of the nations of Europe are bilingual or even multilingual
with two or more ethnic groups speaking different languages.
This is also true for the countries of Africa, Latin America,
and Asia, as well as other places throughout the world. One
does not even need to look so far away from home, since the
national policy of Canada is one of bilingualism. Both French
and English are official languages with a significant portion
of the population being capable of functioning competently in
both languages (Lieberson, 1970).

Although monolingualism is clearly characteristic of the
United States in general, even here English must be considered a second language for a variety of different people. In
New York city, Spanish is the language of the home for many
individuals of Puerto Rican background and it is also a common
first language for many people of Mexican or South American
origin throughout the Southwest. In northern New England it
is not unusual for French to be used in the home. For a variety of Indian populations throughout the country, the native
Indian language has been retained and is sometimes used for

within-group communication. Additionally, within our borders
there are immigrant populations from countries throughout the
world who have retained their native languages and pass them
on to their children. For some children from these ethnic or
cultural subgroups, English is not fully acquired as a second
language until the time of entering school.

Until recently, the prevailing "melting-pot" concept, as
well as a lack of complete understanding of the social significance of language, has usually led to the assumption that
such individuals or ethnic groups will (or should) eventually
give up their native language and join the "more natural" monolingual English-speaking population. This seems to have been
true despite the fact that for the majority of its speakers,
English is a second language throughout the world. Now, however, the United States appears to have begun to recognize the
value of cultural diversity, as well as its relation to linguistic diversity, and is becoming increasingly aware of what
it would be sacrificing if it were to work toward the total
enculturation of such groups. New educational programs that
are intended to preserve and nurture what remains of such cultural diversity reflect this new "enlightened" approach. Because of the close relation which exists between language and
culture, this approach must pay particular attention to the
questions of second-language acquisition and consequent bilingualism. The Bilingual American Education Act of 1967 reflects the increasing awareness of the need for programs that
are aimed at the improvement of education through the use of
bilingual approaches (cf. John & Horner, 1971). If this means,
as it would seem to, that a significantly greater portion of
the population will be expected and even encouraged to continue this tendency toward bilingualism, then it is clearly important that we achieve a greater awareness of the potential
effects of speaking more than one language.

The consideration of the psychological and social implications of bilingualism is thus a significant national issue
and, more broadly, it is also an issue of international importance. Language planning throughout the world is a matter of
educational, political, and social significance. New language
policies will be developed and old policies revised, and in
most instances these will involve issues of bilingualism or
multilingualism. For these reasons, as well as for the additional insight into the general workings of language in the
individual and the society that will undoubtedly result, research into the potential effects of bilingualism is both interesting and important. The chapters that follow represent a
consideration of some of the major current research questions
and findings that bear in diverse ways on this issue.

Before turning to these works, however, it may be advan-
tageous to consider a number of basic concepts and issues that

seem to underly much of the current work on bilingualism as well as to consider some of the historical developments in this area. These represent what I have garnered from my own review of the literature, and I make no claim for their originality or exhaustiveness. As a psycholinguist who has only recently begun to explore the area of bilingualism, this background has proven valuable to me.

VARIETIES AND TYPES OF BILINGUALISM

To be considered bilingual, a person must have the ability to use two different languages, whereas the term multilingual is usually reserved for individuals possessing the ability to use more than two languages. This deceptively simple definition of bilingualism may seem perfectly adequate for general usage; however, it leaves open several issues that have been a constant source of confusion and lack of clarity in the theoretical and research literature on this topic. For example, some writers, like Bloomfield (1933), maintain that the term should be applied only to those individuals who possess "nativelike" ability in both languages, while others (e.g., Haugen, 1956) take the opposite view that bilingualism should be characterized by minimal rather than maximal qualifications. Weinreich (1953, p. 1) takes a more neutral position in defining bilingualism as the "practice of alternatively using two languages." The best way to deal with this variation in definitions would seem to be to recognize that bilingualism is not an all-or-none property, but is an individual characteristic that may exist to degrees varying from minimal competency to complete mastery of more than one language. Thus the problem of evaluating the degree of bilingualism emerges and is an extremely important consideration in questions of research investigation with bilinguals. Such evaluation is complicated, however, by the fact that any system that is intended to be employed for evaluating bilingual competence must take into account the degree of competence in both comprehension and production in the spoken as well as the written mode (Mackey, 1962). Such an evaluative system would also have to consider the relative competence of the individual in the numerous stylistic variations in the speech code that characterize a native speaker (cf. Joos, 1959). Unfortunately no such comprehensive system has yet been developed. Some clarification has been brought to this issue by the introduction of the term "balanced bilingual" (Lambert, Havelka, & Gardener, 1959) which is intended to be used to refer to individuals fully competent in both languages. This, however, is more of an ideal than a fact, since most bilinguals are probably more fluent and more at ease in one of their languages than in the other. For this

reason, the commonly employed convention of listing the domi-
nant language first is followed throughout the present work.
Thus, a French-English bilingual should not be confused with an
English-French bilingual.

Methods of evaluating the degree of dominance (Lambert et
al., 1959; Mackey, 1962) as well as considerations of the factors that may contribute to determining such dominance have
frequently occupied researchers in this area. Many factors may
potentially affect the relative status or strength of an individual's two or more languages, such as: age and order of acquisition, usefulness and amount of opportunity for communication, degree of emotional involvement, social function, as well
as literary and cultural value (Weinreich, 1953). Thus, in exploring the effects of bilingualism it is extremely important
to consider the degree of competence in the second language as
a variable that may significantly affect research results.
This issue is considered in the present volume by Lambert
(Chapter 2) and is the specific focus of investigation in some
of the research reported by Segalowitz and Gatbonton (Chapter
6) as well as Taylor (Chapter 5).

A second issue regarding the problem of defining bilingualism is the question of what actually constitutes "different
languages." A variety of factors relating to historical, sociocultural, political, and geographic considerations have usually been employed in attempting to determine whether two linguistic varieties should properly be considered as distinct
languages, or whether certain variations might better be characterized as dialectical variations (Lyons, 1968). In addition, distinct codes (Bernstein, 1961) or simple stylistic
differences (Joos, 1959) within a single language have often
been taken as significant linguistic variations (cf. Hymes,
1974). Here again, the issue would seem to be one of degree.
At one extreme an individual might be fluent in two languages
from distinctly different language families (e.g., Finnish and
German) or he might simply possess more than one stylistic
variation of the same language (e.g., casual versus formal
English). Bilingualism has sometimes been defined to include
the latter group. For example, Taylor (1976, p. 239) defines
a bilingual as a person who speaks two or more "languages, dialects, or styles of speech that involve differences in sound,
vocabulary and syntax." Under this definition, most normal
adult speakers of any language would be considered bilingual.
The important question, however, is whether or not a single
theoretical model such as that suggested by Hymes (1967, 1974)
should be applied to all such code variation. It may well be
the case that many of the phenomena and effects related to bilingualism are equally characteristic of other forms of code
variations (see, e.g., Bernstein, 1961; Labov, 1966); however,
the present work is focused on the bilingual situation in which

two distinct language competencies are present in the same individual, what Hymes (1974, p. 30) has referred to as "bilingualism par excellence."

One of the ways in which bilingualism par excellence (e.g., speakers of both French and English in Canada or Welsh and English in Wales) may differ significantly from stylistic variation is related to the question of the degree of cultural variation or cultural duality associated with the differences in linguistic codes. As pointed out by Pride (1971), there is a very important distinction between bilingualism and biculturalism, and although they may frequently occur together, they can also occur separately. The possession of two stylistic variations of English or two dialectical variations of Dutch is not necessarily associated with significant cultural variation. However, since in many cases possession of two languages does reflect interaction and knowledge of distinct cultures, it is important to realize the fact that many of the effects commonly associated with bilingualism may actually reflect the result of such concomitant biculturalism. The importance of this distinction is reflected in part by the widespread use of the distinction between compound and coordinate bilingualism identified by Weinreich (1953). While this distinction has proven to be somewhat slippery, it has generally been taken to reflect the degree of semantic overlap between the two language systems within the individual. Coordinate bilinguals are considered to have separate (and different) semantic systems, while compound bilinguals are taken to simply have two distinct modes of expression (the two languages) for a single underlying semantic network. Although a variety of factors have been related to this distinction and it has been a topic of considerable research (see Lambert, 1969, for a review), a number of studies (Lambert, Havelka, & Crosby, 1958; Lambert & Rawlings, 1969; Kolers, 1963; Ervin-Tripp, 1964; and others) suggest that the question of whether the languages have been learned in two geographically separate cultural contexts may be the variable of prime significance in determining the so-called compound-coordinate distinction. It must be pointed out that this variable is probably confounded with age of acquisition, since individuals acquiring two languages in infancy are more likely to do so in the same cultural context than those individuals acquiring a second language at a later time. After reviewing the relevant literature in this area, Taylor (1976, p. 261) concludes that "The distinction between coordinate and compound bilingualism . . . is neither clear-cut nor useful." Although discussion of this issue has contributed significantly to the literature on bilingualism, its lack of usefulness is becoming increasingly clear and as such it is not dealt with to any great degree in the present volume. The more important factor that seems to underly this presumed distinction is the presence

or absence of biculturalism. The degree of biculturalism possessed by a bilingual speaker is a major factor to consider in
dealing with bilingual research. The importance of this consideration is brought out in the work of Lambert (Chapter 2)
and Taylor (Chapter 5), and the orientation throughout the present work is predominantly toward the consideration of bilingualism within a bicultural setting. However, it must be pointed
out that such biculturalism does not necessarily mean a total
or even significant separation of linguistic systems within
the individual (as was intended by the older notion of coordinate bilingualism). This is supported by the research on bilingual memory reviewed by McCormack in Chapter 4, and it is also
the conclusion reached by Segalowitz (in press) regarding the
unity of the semantic system underlying two or more languages.
    The possible relation between the compound-coordinate dis-
tinction and another issue of sociological significance, diglossia, has been discussed by Fishman (1965). This term,
originally introduced by Ferguson (1959), is used to refer to
those situations in which two or more languages are used differentially within a single geographic region. Gumperz (1966)
has extended this concept to include variations in dialect,
register, or variety and thus comes to the inevitable conclusion that almost all societies possess diglossia to some extent. One language, dialect, variety, etc., will normally be
used for some social functions (e.g., education, government,
religion, family interaction, work) while a distinctly different linguistic variety may be employed for the remaining social functions. To the extent that these social functions and
roles are occupied by distinct social groups, then such diglossic situations are often associated with the existence of
separate-language-speaking populations within the same geographic community. This distinction is often between a high
and low variety or language (e.g., between High and Low German). With regard to the content of the present volume, the
important point to be made is that diglossia is a characteristic of societies or social groups, whereas bilingualism is a
characteristic of individuals. As outlined by Fishman (1967),
the theoretically independent relationship between diglossia
and bilingualism makes it possible to consider four potentially different types of situations with individuals being either
bilingual or monolingual in a social context that may either
possess or not possess diglossia. Thus, in a diglossic society,
some of the members may be monolingual in one of the languages,
some in the other, while a third group may be bilingual and
capable of functioning comfortably in either group or social
setting. Thus, for example, in the now officially bilingual
country of Canada, a 1961 demographic study revealed that more
than 65 percent of the population was monolingual in English,
about 20 percent of the population was monolingual in French,
and only about 12 percent of the population was actually clas-

sified as bilingual (Lieberson, 1970). The relationship between diglossia and bilingualism is quite complex, however,
with these dimensions really being only theoretically separ-
able. As Fishman (1967) points out, societies in which widespread bilingualism exists will tend to move toward diglossia,
and in almost all diglossic societies there will be some individuals who for economic, political, geographic, or other reasons will form a link between the two speech communities and
hence will have to be bilingual. With regard to the orientation of the present volume, it must be stressed that here we
are interested primarily in the effects of bilingualism (a
characteristic of the individual) rather than the socially and
personally significant effects of diglossia (a characteristic
of the linguistic organization at the sociocultural level).
Many of the political, economic, emotional, and social problems typically related to bilingualism should probably more
properly be considered as the result of diglossia (see, e.g.,
Inglehart & Woodward, 1967) and thus are beyond the scope of
the present volume. In fact, it may well be the case that it
is the absence of widespread bilingualism in an otherwise diglossic community that leads to social and political unrest.
Factors that lead to the promotion of functional bilingualism
in such contexts are thus an extremely important area of study.
Some of the important considerations in this regard are dealt
with by Taylor (Chapter 5) and to some extent also by Fishman,
Cooper, and Rosenbaum (Chapter 8) and Tucker (Chapter 9).

The presence of diglossia is also an important contextual
factor in considering the implications of bilingualism. Fishman (1972, p. 104) has pointed out that "many of the purported
'disadvantages' of bilingualism have been falsely generalized
to the phenomenon at large rather than related to the absence
or presence of social patterns that reach substantially beyond
bilingualism." The presence or absence of diglossia is however, only one distinction among a variety of potential social
settings in which the bilingual individual may find himself.
In fact, Stewart (1968) has developed a typology for describing
multilingualism that distinguishes ten separate social functions that a second language may serve which range from an official, legally appropriate language for all activities to a
language used in connection with the ritual of a particular religion. Since bilingualism always occurs within some particular social setting, the potential effects that it will have on
the individual may vary widely depending on the particular social significance and function of the two languages. Consideration of this factor is involved in the distinction between
"additive" and "subtractive" bilingualism introduced by Lambert
(Chapter 2) and is considered in great detail by Fishman (Chapter 8) in relation to the existence of English as a second language for a large number of people throughout the world.

Bilingual individuals thus differ considerably in terms of their degree of competence in their two languages (balanced versus dominant), in the linguistic relationship between the two speech varieties (distinct languages versus stylistic variations), in the degree of cultural duality involved (bilingualism versus biculturalism), and in the sociocultural significance or function of the languages involved, as well as other possible sources of variation. These factors might be viewed as serious impediments to progress in this field of investigation since they severely restrict the extent to which even the clearest research results can be generalized to other settings. However, it is undoubtedly more valuable to treat such variation as a natural laboratory in which it may be possible to study the separate and interactive effects of these diverse factors in order to determine their influences on the psychological and social behavior of the individual. The difficulty of doing research in such naturalistic settings should not, however, be underestimated. Since it appears that bilingualism is a fact of life, the important practical contribution of such research will be in the direction of discovering those characteristics of the bilingual setting which determine whether bilingualism will be a source of enrichment and diversity, and hence desirable, or a source of frustration and confusion, and thus to be avoided.

THE PRESENT VOLUME: A MULTIDISCIPLINARY APPROACH

From the preceding discussion it should be clear that the contributions to the present volume are wide ranging and diverse and encompass many issues traditionally associated with a number of different areas of study. This is because bilingualism, like any other important social or behavioral phenomenon, does not fall neatly within the boundaries of any single discipline. Although the study of language and languages (and hence bilingualism) may traditionally have been the province of linguists, several recent developments over the past two decades have resulted in a greatly increasing interest in this area on the part of several of the behavioral sciences including psychology, sociology, and education. The newly developed fields of psycholinguistics and sociolinguistics, as well as the general trend toward increased interest in applied linguistics have not failed to consider bilingualism in their efforts to understand the diverse ways in which language and behavior interact.

From the viewpoint of linguistics, bilingualism is, however, still of considerable interest because of its important role in the determination of historical changes in language systems. When speakers of different languages come into contact for extended periods of time, significant changes in one or both of the language systems involved invariably result. The emergence of Middle English as a result of the Norman invasion of England is a well-known example. Because of the interference that normally occurs between first and second languages within the individual, the bilingual speaker plays a significant role in this regard.

Bilingualism affects much more than the languages involved, however, and psychologists and sociologists are exploring many facets of its effects on the individual and the society. At the psychological level there are a number of key issues including such considerations as the effects which speaking or knowing two languages might have on one's intellectual functioning, how belonging to two language communities might affect one's personality and sense of identity, and the effects of bilingualism on one's perception and social interaction with others. Since the new field of sociolinguistics has as its main focus the question of the relationship between the social structure and the linguistic organization of the society, the language variation introduced by the presence of more than one language falls clearly within this domain. The social meaning and significance of variations in speech codes is thus an important issue in the sociology of language.

Because of the primary role of language as a medium of instruction, and because of the close relationship between verbal functioning and measured intelligence, bilingualism has also not been neglected by those interested in the field of education, particularly at the primary grade levels. Such basic questions as the determination of which of the two languages will be the language of instruction in a bilingual community, or whether classes in both languages should be available, have been major concerns in recent years. The goal of increasing competency in the weaker of the two languages through second-language teaching is also an important concern of educators.

The preceding issues in linguistics, psychology, sociology, and education are among the primary concerns of the present volume. Although many of these issues can be traced back to the pioneering work of Weinreich (1953), who brought together the diverse literature in existence at that time, the research efforts of the past quarter of a century put us in such a position that we are now able to begin to provide some clear answers to many of these questions.

The individual contributions to the present volume are organized into three overlapping but distinct focuses of concern: the consequences of bilingualism at the level of the individual, the effects of bilingualism on social interaction and the society, and the significance of bilingualism at the national and international levels.

Chapters 2, 3, and 4 deal primarily with individual as-

pects of bilingualism. Lambert's chapter traces the study of
the effects of bilingualism on intelligence, beginning with the
early work in the 1920s and continuing up to the present time.
Much of the progress in this area is the direct result of Lambert's own work and that of his associates. This paper also
includes a comprehensive discussion of the relation between bilingualism and intellectual creativity as well as its effects
on personality and identity. Ben-Zeev's contribution is based
in part on her research on the intellectual processes of bilingual children in Israel, in New York city, and elsewhere. Taking primarily a cognitive-linguistic orientation, Ben-Zeev has
investigated the specific ways in which acquiring more than one
language may affect an individual's language development as
well as its effect on general cognitive style and capacity for
learning. Still staying within the area of intellectual functioning, but turning to bilingual adults, McCormack deals with
the question of the bilingual's storage and recall of verbal
information. McCormack reviews the major research findings in
this area, including some of his own work, and provides some
new interpretations which may resolve a considerable amount of
confusion resulting from the seemingly conflicting findings in
this area.

In considering some of the more social aspects of bilingualism, Chapters 5, 6, and 7 include Taylor's work on the social interaction of bilingual speakers. Taylor is concerned
with the fact that in bilingual communities intergroup relations are often considerably limited and uncomfortable. The
question of the reasons for this limited interaction as well
as possible means of promoting or improving such exchanges are
considered. Segalowitz and Gatbonton, who are also interested
in social attitudes and behavior, focus their attention on the
nonfluent bilingual. Such questions as whether or not nonfluent speakers of a second language constitute a speech community
in the linguistic sense, how such individuals might react to
situations calling for stylistic variations that are not in
their repertoire, and how native speakers of the second language perceive and react to such nonfluent speakers are among
their chief concerns. Social and personal attitudes are also
reflected in Haugen's contribution. This chapter considers
the question of what constitutes normal linguistic usage in a
bilingual community. Since minority group language behavior
and practices will invariably be affected by the language patterns of the dominant population, the question of how these
changes might be dealt with and reacted to by the minority language speakers is among Haugen's main concerns.

Chapters 8 and 9 comprise that section of the volume which
deals with some of the significant national and international
aspects of the phenomenon of bilingualism. Fishman, Cooper,
and Rosenbaum report the results of their comprehensive study

that was designed to determine the relative importance of a variety of factors that have led to the spread of English as a second language throughout the world today. More than fifty different variables are studied in attempting to determine their contribution to this significant factor in the creation of worldwide bilingualism. In Chapter 9, Tucker, drawing on his experience and research in the Philippines, the Middle East, Nigeria, the Maghreb, and Haiti, presents a discussion of the current trends in the use of indigenous languages as a medium of instruction in the public schools in these bilingual societies. A variety of factors including an increased desire for functional literacy, more universal primary education, and increased ethnic and national identity are related to this important educational issue. Tucker also discusses recent trends in Canada and the United States in this regard.

The final summary and discussion chapter by Genesee, whose own current interests focus on the cognitive and educational aspects of bilingualism, is intended to tie together some of the diverse threads that run throughout the previous chapters and to put the individual contributions into focus within the larger perspective of the general implications of bilingualism for the individual and for the society.

REFERENCES

Bernstein, B. Social structure, language and learning.
    Educational Research, 1961, *3,* 163-176.
Bloomfield, L. *Language.* New York: Holt, Rinehart and
    Winston, 1933.
Ervin-Tripp, S. An analysis of the interaction of language,
    topic, and listener. *American Anthropologist,* 1964, *66,*
    86-102.
Ferguson, C.A. Diglossia. *Word,* 1959, *15,* 325-340.
Fishman, J.A. Who speaks what language to whom and when?
    Linguistigue, 1965, *2,* 67-88.
Fishman, J.A. Bilingualism with and without diglossia; di-
    glossia with and without bilingualism. In J. Macnamara
    (Ed.), Problems of Bilingualism. *The Journal of Social
    Issues,* 1967, *23,* 29-38.
Fishman, J.A. *The sociology of language.* Rowley, Mass.:
    Newbury House, 1972.
Gumperz, J.J. On the ethnography of linguistic change.
    In W. Bright (Ed.), *Sociolinguistics.* The Hague:
    Mouton, 1966. Pp. 27-38.
Haugen, E. *Bilingualism in the Americas: A bibliography
    and a research guide.* Montgomery: University of
    Alabama Press, 1956.

Hymes, D.   Models of the interaction of language and social
setting. In J. Macnamara (Ed.), Problems of Bilingualism.
The Journal of Social Issues, 1967, 23, (2), 8-28.
Hymes, D.   Foundations in sociolinguistics. Philadelphia:
University of Pennsylvania Press, 1974.
Inglehart, R., & Woodward, M.   Language conflicts and the
political community. In P.P. Giglioli (Ed.), Language
and social context. London: Penguin Books, 1972.
John, V.P., & Horner, V.M.   Early childhood bilingual educa-
tion. New York: Modern Language Association of America,
1971.
Joos, M.   The isolation of styles. In R. Harrell (Ed.),
Report of the 10th round table meeting. Washington,
D.C.: Georgetown University Press, 1959, Pp. 107-113.
Kolers, P.A.   Interlingual word associations. Journal of
Verbal Learning and Verbal Behavior, 1963, 2, 291-300.
Labov, W.   The social stratification of English in New York
City. Washington, D.C.: Center for Applied Linguistics,
1966.
Lambert, W.E.   Psychological studies of the interdependencies
of the bilingual's two languages. In J. Puhvel (Ed.),
Substance and structure of language. Los Angeles:
University of California Press, 1969, Pp. 99-126.
Lambert, W.E., Havelka, J. & Crosby, C.   The influence of
language acquisition contexts on bilingualism. Journal
of Abnormal and Social Psychology, 1958, 56, 239-244.
Lambert, W.E., Havelka, J. & Gardner, R.C.   Linguistic Mani-
festations of Bilingualism. American Journal of Psy-
chology, 1959, 72, 77-82.
Lambert, W.E. & Rawlings, C.   Bilingual processing of mixed-
language associative networks.Journal of Verbal Learning
and Verbal Behavior, 1969, 8, 604-609.
Lieberson, S.   Language and ethnic relations in Canada.
New York: Wiley, 1970.
Lyons, J.   Introduction to theoretical linguistics.
Cambridge: Cambridge University Press, 1968.
Mackey, W.F.   The description of bilingualism. Canadian
Journal of Linguistics, 1962, 7, 51-85.
Pride, J.B.   The social meaning of language. Oxford:
Oxford University Press, 1971.
Segalowitz, N.   Psychological perspectives on bilingual edu-
cation. In B. Spolsky and R.L. Cooper (Eds.), Fron-
tiers of bilingual education. Rowley, Mass.: New-
bury House (in press).
Stewart, W.A.   Sociolinguistic typology of multilingualism.
In J. Fishman (Ed.), Readings in the sociology of lan-
guage. The Hague: Mouton, 1968, Pp. 531-545.

Taylor, I. *Introduction to psycholinguistics*. New York: Holt, Rinehart and Winston, 1976.

Weinreich, U. *Languages in contact*. New York: Linguistic Circle of New York, 1953.

Chapter 2

The Effects of Bilingualism
on the Individual: Cognitive
and Sociocultural Consequences

WALLACE E. LAMBERT

McGill University

The still growing technical literature on the consequences
of becoming bilingual and/or bicultural stretches back to the
turn of the century. In the early literature (the 1920s and
1930s) we find a generally pessimistic outlook on the effects
of bilingualism, but since the 1960s a much more optimistic
picture has been emerging. Bilingualism and biculturalism, as
one might expect, generate much emotional and political steam
and this often clouds whatever facts are available. Researchers in the early period generally expected to find all sorts
of troubles, and they usually did: bilingual children, relative
to monolinguals, were behind in school, retarded in measured
intelligence, and socially adrift. One trouble with most of
the early studies was that little care was taken to check out
the essentials before comparing monolingual and bilingual subjects. Thus, such factors as social class background and educational opportunities were not controlled, nor was much attention given to determining how bilingual or monolingual the comparison groups actually were. But even though there were
grounds for worrying about the adequacy of many of these studies, the results, nonetheless, were remarkably clear: the
largest proportion of these investigations concluded that bilingualism has a detrimental effect on intellectual functioning; a smaller number found little or no relation between bilingualism and intelligence; and only two suggested that bilingualism might have favorable effects on cognition.
    With this picture as background, Elizabeth Peal and I
started an investigation on the bilingual-monolingual topic in
1962 in the Canadian setting. We had, of course, strong expec-
tations of finding a bilingual deficit, as the literature sug-

15

gested, but we wanted to pinpoint what the intellectual components of that deficit might be in order to develop compensatory strategies. We argued that a large proportion of the world's population is, by the exigencies of life, bound to be bilingual, and it seemed to us appropriate to help them, if possible. Thus we expected troubles, but didn't find any.

We were able in our first investigation to overcome most of the shortcomings noted in the earlier research, making us feel relatively confident about the results (see Lambert & Anisfeld, 1969). What surprised us, though, was that French-English bilingual children in the Montreal setting scored significantly ahead of carefully matched monolinguals on both verbal and nonverbal measures of intelligence. Furthermore, the patterns of test results suggested that the bilinguals had a more diversified structure of intelligence, as measured, and more flexibility in thought.

These results, suggesting the possibility that bilingualism might favorably affect the structure and flexibility of thought, came as a real surprise. But one investigation rarely has enough weight to change the course of events, even though an important follow-up study (Anisfeld, 1964) confirmed the 1962 conclusions. What was needed was confirmation from other settings and from studies using different approaches. Fortunately, since then confirmations have started to emerge from carefully conducted research around the world, from Singapore (Torrance, Gowan, Wu, & Aliotti, 1970), Switzerland (Balkan, 1970), South Africa (Ianco-Worrall, 1972), Israel and New York (Ben-Zeev, 1972), western Canada (Cummins & Gulutsan, 1973), and, using a quite different approach, from Montreal (Scott, 1973). All of these studies (and we found no others in the recent literature to contradict them) indicate that bilingual children, relative to monolingual controls, show definite advantages on measures of "cognitive flexibility," "creativity," or "divergent thought." Sandra Ben-Zeev's study, for example, involved Hebrew-English bilingual children in New York and Israel and the results strongly support the conclusion that bilinguals have greater "cognitive flexibility." In this case, the term means that bilinguals have greater "skill at auditory reorganization" of verbal material, a much more "flexible manipulation of the linguistic code," and more advanced performance on tests of "concrete operational thinking" as these were measured in her investigation. Anita Ianco-Worrall's study involved Afrikaans-English bilingual children in Pretoria, South Africa, and it lends equally strong support for a somewhat different form of cognitive flexibility, an advantage over monolingual controls in separating word meaning from word sound. The conclusion is drawn that the bilinguals were between two and three years advanced in this feature of cognitive development which Leopold (1949) felt to be so characteristic of the

liberated thought of bilinguals. Worrall also found good support for a bilingual precocity in realizing the arbitrary as-
signment of names to referents, a feature of thinking which
Vygotsky (1962) believed reflected insight and sophistication.

A study by Sheridan Scott (1973) of French-English bilinguals in Montreal is perhaps the most persuasive because it involved a comparison of young children, some of whom were given
the chance to become bilingual over a period of years and others who were not given the chance. She worked with data collected over a seven-year period from two groups of English-
Canadian children, one group that had become functionally bilingual in French during the time period because they had attended experimental classes where most of the instruction had
been conducted in French, while the other group had followed a
conventional English-language education program. At the grade
1 level, the two groups had been equated for measured intelligence, socioeconomic background, and parental attitudes toward
French people. In fact, had the opportunity been presented to
them, it is likely that most of the parents in the control
group would have enrolled their children in the experimental
French program, but since it was decided in advance to start
one experimental class per year only (see Lambert & Tucker,
1972) no such opportunity was available.

Scott was interested in the possible effects that becoming bilingual might have on the cognitive development of children, in particular, what effect it would have on children's
"divergent thinking," a special type of cognitive flexibility
(see Guilford, 1950, 1956). In contrast, convergent thinking
is measured by tests that provide a number of pieces of information which the subject must synthesize to arrive at a correct
answer; thus, the information provided funnels in or converges
on a correct solution. Measures of divergent thinking provide
the subject with a starting point for thought — "think of a
paper clip" — and ask the subject to generate a whole series of
permissible solutions — "and tell me all the things one could
do with it." Some researchers have considered divergent thinking as an index of creativity (e.g., Getzels & Jackson, 1962)
while others suggest that until more is known it is best viewed
as a distinctive cognitive style reflecting a rich imagination
and an ability to scan rapidly a host of possible solutions.

Scott was interested, among other things, in whether bilingualism promotes divergent thinking. Her results, based on
a multivariate analysis, show that the group of youngsters who
had become functionally bilingual through "immersion" schooling
were substantially higher scorers than the monolingual group
with whom they had been equated for IQ and social class background at the first grade level. Although the numbers of children in each group are small, this study gives strong support
for the causal link between bilingualism and flexibility, the

former apparently enhancing the latter.

There is then an impressive array of evidence accumulating that argues plainly against the common sense notion that becoming bilingual, i.e., having two strings to one's bow or two linguistic systems within one's brain, naturally divides a person's cognitive resources and reduces his efficiency of thought. Instead one can now put forth a very persuasive argument that there is a definite cognitive advantage enjoyed by bilingual children in the domain of cognitive flexibility. Only further research will tell us how this advantage, assuming it is a reliable phenomenon, actually works: whether it is based on a better storage of information by bilinguals, whether the separation of linguistic symbols from their referents or the ability to separate word meaning from word sound is the key factor, whether the bilingual contrasts of linguistic systems aid in the development of general conceptual thought, or whatever. In any case, this new trend in research should give second thoughts to those who have used the bilingual deficit notion as an argument for melting down ethnic groups. Hopefully, too, it will provide a new perspective for members of ethnolinguistic groups who may have been led to believe in the notion of a likely deficit attributable to bilingualism.

Because of its social significance, there is a great need for more research on this topic. An example of research to come is presented by Cummins (1976) who is intrigued by differences in findings of pre- and post-1960 studies. Cummins argues that perhaps because the more recent studies have all examined the degrees of two-language skills the subjects actually have (a neglected matter in the earlier work), there may therefore "be a threshold level of linguistic competence which a bilingual child must attain both in order to avoid cognitive deficits and to allow the potentially beneficial aspects of becoming bilingual to influence his cognitive functioning." This would suggest, among other things, that linguistic minority groups need assurance that the *home* language will be given a strong reading and writing base before or along with the introduction of the national language. It is a potentially productive hypothesis to test.

One feature of the studies just reviewed merits special attention: all the cases reported (those in Singapore, South Africa, Switzerland, Israel, New York, Montreal) dealt with bilinguals for whom the two languages involved have social value and respect in each of the settings. Thus, knowing Afrikaans and English in South Africa, Hebrew and English in New York and Israel, or French as well as English for English-speaking Canadian children would in each case be adding a second, socially relevant language to one's repertory of skills. In no case would the learning of the second language portend the slow replacement of it for the home or the other language, as would typically be the case for French Canadians or Spanish Americans developing high-level skills in English. We might refer to these as examples of an "additive" form of bilingualism and contrast it with a more "subtractive" form experienced by many ethnic minority groups who because of national educational policies and social pressures of various sorts are forced to put aside their ethnic language for a national language. Their degree of bilinguality at any time would be likely to reflect some stage in the subtraction of the ethnic language and the associated culture, and their replacement with another. The important educational task of the future, it seems to me, is to transfer the pressures on ethnic groups so that they can profit from additive forms of bilingualism and biculturalism. We'll present an example of an attempt to make such a transformation in the last section.

EFFECTS ON IDENTITY

What about the notion that becoming bilingual and bicultural subtracts, through division, from one's sense of personal identity? Here too, there are signs in the recent literature of interest in this topic, but there are still only a few studies to draw on. Three, however, do bear on the issue of the identity of bilinguals, and all three are encouraging in their outcomes.

The first is the study that Robert Gardner and I conducted with French Americans in communities in New England and Louisiana (Gardner & Lambert, 1972). We were interested in their ways of coping with a dual heritage, and we found that some oriented themselves definitely toward their French background and tried to ignore their American roots; others were tugged more toward the American pole at the expense of their Frenchness; and still others apparently tried not to think in ethnic terms, as though they did not consider themselves as being either French or American. These three types of reactions parallel closely those of Italian-American adolescents studied earlier by Child (1943). To me these ways of coping characterize the anguish of members of ethnic groups when caught up in a subtractive form of biculturalism, that is, where social pressures (often from within their own group) are exerted on them to give up one aspect of their dual identity for the sake of blending into a national scene. The important point here is that identities are fragile and they can, through social pressures, be easily tipped off balance. Thus, some of these young people were trying to be one thing or the other while others were trying to be neither one thing nor the other. Most interesting was our finding of a fourth subgroup of French-American young people who were apparently successful at being *both* things, French and American. This subgroup was characterized by a realization of the social usefulness of knowing French which was given strong parental support. The pattern suggested that this familywide orientation toward the value of French helped these young people become relatively more competent in both French and English.

Identities need not be disturbed, though, as the study of Aellen & Lambert (1969) showed. In this case we were interested in the adjustments made by adolescent children of English-French mixed marriages in the Montreal setting. We examined the degree and direction of the offspring's ethnic identifications as well as a selected set of their attitudes and personality characteristics.

The children of these mixed marriages come in contact with and are usually expected to learn the distinctive social and behavioral characteristics of the two cultures represented in their families. The question is whether the demands made on them necessarily generate conflicts, whether the experience with two cultures possibly broadens and liberalizes the child, or whether some combination of both outcomes is typical. In addition to the cultural demands made on them, the children of mixed ethnic marriages may face other difficulties to the extent that their parents, as suggested by Gordon (1966) and Saucier (1965), may have married outside their ethnic group because of personal instability and immaturity. Much of the previous research suggests that persons who intermarry in this way often have relatively strong feelings of alienation, self-hatred, and worthlessness, and are disorganized and demoralized. Mixed ethnic children might well find it difficult to identify with their parents if these characteristics are typical or representative. Still, the offspring could develop understanding and sympathy for parents with such an outlook. On the other hand, people may intermarry in many instances because they have developed essentially healthy attitudes and orientations which are nonetheless inappropriate within their own ethnic group, making intermarriage with a sympathetic outsider particularly attractive. They may have become, like Park's marginal man, "the individual with the wider horizon, the keener intelligence, the more detached and rational viewpoint... always relatively the more civilized human being" (Park, 1964, p. 376). In that case, their children might be particularly well trained in tolerance and openmindedness, especially since the children, themselves, are likely to feel that they, unlike their parents, are automatically members of both ethnic groups. The purpose of this investigation was to examine both of these possibilities as objectively as possible by comparing groups of adolescent boys of mixed French-English parentage with others of homogeneous background, either French or English. All groups in the comparison were similar as to age, socioeconomic class, intelligence, and number of siblings.

It was found that the profile of characteristics of the boys with mixed ethnic parentage is a healthy one in every respect when comparisons are made with groups from homogeneous ethnic backgrounds; they identify with their parents, especially with their fathers, as well as the comparison groups do; they relate themselves to and identify with both ethnic reference groups, this being particularly so for those in a French academic environment; they show no signs of personality disturbances, social alienation, or anxiety; nor do their self-concepts deviate from those of the comparison subjects; they see their parents as giving them relatively more attention and showing more personal interest in them, and their attitudes toward parents are as favorable as those of the comparison groups; they seek out distinctively affectionate relationships with peers; their general attitudinal orientations are similar to those of the comparison groups while their specific attitudes toward both English and French Canadians are relatively unbiased; their values show the influence of both ethnic backgrounds as do their achievement orientations which are less extreme than those of the comparison groups. Rather than developing a divided allegiance or repressing one or both aspects of their backgrounds, as has been noted among the offspring of certain immigrant groups (Child, 1943), they apparently have developed a dual allegiance that permits them to identify with both their parents, and to feel that they themselves are wanted as family members. One of the mixed ethnic boys summed up this finding by saying: "I respect both my parents, and I respect their origins." One might argue that the concern of the parents of mixed ethnic adolescents to "include" their children is exaggerated, a symptom of tension and value conflict, but such an interpretation is negated by the apparent success these parents have had in passing on a sense of being wanted. There are, however, many features of this pattern of results that need further study.

This profile sketch is more characteristic of the mixed ethnic subjects who are part of the French-Canadian high school environment. These young people may be more susceptible to the English-Canadian culture than those attending English-Canadian schools would be to French-Canadian culture because of the Canadian cultural tug of war which seems, at least until recently to be controlled by the more powerful and prestigious English-Canadian communities (see Lambert, 1967).

Two general modes of adjustment to a mixed ethnic background became apparent. In one case, these young men incorporate both ethnic streams of influence, which are either modified by the parents before they are passed on to their children, or are tempered by the adolescents themselves, so that they are less extreme than those represented by either of the major reference groups. A tendency to amalgamate both cultural streams of influence is suggested by the contrasts noted between the ethnically mixed groups and the homogeneous groups, e.g., the unbiased ethnic identifications of the former, their percep- tions of parents as being inclusive, their favorable attitudes toward both English and French Canadians, and their less ex- treme achievement values. In the other case, they tend to adapt their views to the predominant features of the academic- cultural environment in which they find themselves. This form of adjustment is suggested by the tendency of the mixed ethnic groups to line up with the respective homogeneous groups with whom they attend high school, e.g., in their choices of the values they hope to pass on to their own children, the person- ality traits they see as desirable, and their judgments of the relative attractiveness of English-Canadian or French-Canadian girls.

This illustration provides hope for biculturality in the sense that offspring of mixed-ethnic marriages appear to profit from the dual cultural influences found in their families. Rather than cultural conflicts, we find well-adjusted young people with broad perspectives who are comfortable in the role of representing both of their cultural backgrounds. We also have here an illustration of the additive form of bicultural- ism; the boys studied were caught in the flow of two cultural streams and were apparently happy to be part of both streams.

There is a similar type outcome in the investigation con- ducted by Richard Tucker and myself (Lambert & Tucker, 1972) concerning the English-Canadian children who took the majority of their elementary schooling via French, and who after grades 5 and 6 had become functionally bilingual. Here we were able to measure on a yearly basis their self-conceptions and their attitudes toward English-Canadian, French-Canadian, and French- French ways of life. The attitude profiles of the children in the Experimental French program indicate that by the fifth grade important affective changes have occurred during the course of the project. The children state that they enjoy the form of education they are receiving and want to stay with it; their feelings toward French people have become decidedly more favorable; and they now think of themselves as being both French Canadian and English Canadian in personal makeup. It is this apparent identification with French people — those from Canada and those from Europe — that raises the question of bi- culturalism. Has the program made the children more bicultur- al? It is difficult to answer this question because the mean- ing of bicultural is so vague. It is certain that the children had come to feel they can be at ease in both French- and Eng- lish-Canadian social settings, and that they were becoming both French and English in certain ways; but not becoming less Eng- lish as a consequence. It is certain too that they have learned that in classes with European-French teachers they should stand when a visitor enters while they need not stand in classes that are conducted by English-Canadian or French-Canadian teachers. We wonder how much more there is to being bicultural beyond knowing thoroughly the languages involved, feeling personally aligned with both groups, and knowing how to behave in the two atmospheres. Are there any deeper personal aspects to cultural differences? That is, does culture actually affect personality all that much or is it perhaps a more superficial and thinner wrapping than many social scientists have suggested?

The attitudes of the parents at the start of the project were basically friendly and favorable, although marked with very little knowledge about the French-Canadian people around them. These parents wanted their children to learn French for what appear to be integrative reasons — getting to know the other ethnic group and their distinctive ways — but they did not want them to go so far as to think and feel as French Canadians do; in other words, they were guarded and did not want their children to lose their English-Canadian identity. How will they interpret the attitudes of their children who by grade 5 come to think of themselves as being both English Canadian and French Canadian in disposition and outlook? Some may see this as a worrisome sign of identity loss, and although we are not optimistic we believe they would, if patient, come to view their children's enjoyment in having both English- and French-Canadian friends and both types of outlooks as a valuable addition, not a subtraction or cancellation of identities. As we see it, the children are acquiring a second social overcoat which seems to increase their interest in dressing up and reduces the monotony of either coat used alone. Our hope is that the children can convince worried parents that the experience is, in fact, enriching and worthwhile, but the pressures against the children doing so are powerful.

These studies suggest to us that there is no basis in reality for the belief that becoming bilingual or bicultural necessarily means a loss or dissolution of identity. We are aware of the possible pressures that can surround members of ethnolinguistic minority groups and make them hesitate to become full-fledged members of two cultural communities. At the same time, though, we see how easy and rewarding it can be for those who are able to capitalize on a nation's dual heritage. The question of most interest, then, is: How in modern societies can these possibilities be extended to ethnolinguistic minority groups?

Actually, very little has been done in North America over the years to help ethnolinguistic minority groups maintain respect in and for their linguistic and cultural heritage so that they could become full-fledged bicultural members of their national societies. There are, however, several recent developments in the American society that hold out a new and exciting type of hope. These developments, in fact, constitute another instance where the United States has an opportunity to set an outstanding example of what can be done for ethnic minority groups. The first development is a new perspective, generated, it seems, by the critical self-analysis of collegiate activists in the 1960s, on what it means to be American. It was American collegiates who demanded national respect for minority groups of every variety, including Afro-Americans and American Indians. As a nation, these young people argued, we have no right to wash out distinctive traditions of any minority group since their ways of life, relative to the so-called American way of life, are in many respects admirable.

The second development, which may have stemmed from the first, takes the form of a national willingness to help minority groups. One way this willingness to help manifests itself is in new educational laws that provide extensive schooling in Spanish for Spanish Americans in America's large centers, in the passage of the Bilingual Education Act, and in new laws passed in states such as Massachusetts which provide schooling in any number of home languages whenever a group of parents request it.

The third development is a new direction in psycholinguistic research which, although only now getting underway, indicates that the hyphenated American can perhaps most easily become fully and comfortably American if the Spanish, the Polish, the Navajo, or the French prefix is given unlimited opportunity to flourish. For example, the research of Padilla and Long (1969; see also Long & Padilla, 1970) suggests that Spanish-American children and adolescents can learn English better and adjust more comfortably to America if their linguistic and cultural ties with the Spanish speaking world are kept alive and active from infancy on. Peal and Lambert (1962) came to a similar conclusion when they found that French-Canadian young people who are given opportunities to become bilingual are more likely than monolinguals to be advanced in their schooling in French schools, to develop a diversified and flexible intelligence, and to develop attitudes that are as charitable toward the other major Canadian cultural group as their own. A similar conclusion is drawn from the recent work of Lambert and Tucker (1972) where English-Canadian youngsters are given most of their elementary training via French. These children too seem to be advanced relatively, in their cognitive development, their appreciation for French people and French ways of life, and their own sense of breadth and depth as Canadians.

In view of these sympathetic and supportive new developments, is it now possible to assist the hyphenated American to become fully and comfortably bilingual and bicultural? Is it

now possible to counteract and change the reactions of ethnically different children in America so that they will no longer feel different, peculiar and inferior whenever they take on
their Spanish, Portuguese, Polish, Navajo, or French styles of
life as temporary replacements for the American style?

Our own thinking on this matter is based on the following
working hypotheses: that in bilingual communities where differential prestige is accorded to the languages and to the ethnolinguistic groups involved, then attention should be placed by
both linguistic groups on the development of skills in the language more likely to be overlooked. Thus, for French Canadians
in Canada rather than exploring early immersion-in-English programs, the French-Canadian community should consolidate and
deepen its control of French, and branch into English-language
training as early as possible, but only as signs appear that
full competence in the potentially neglected home language is
assured. In this way trends toward subtractive forms of bilingualism or biculturalism can be transformed into additive ones.

An American example of this sort of transformation is the
case of French Americans in northern New England who have recently been given a chance to be schooled partly in their home
language (Dubé & Herbert, 1975a, 1975b; Lambert, Giles, & Picard, 1975; Lambert, Giles, & Albert, 1974). In the northern
regions of Maine, some 85 percent of families have kept French
alive as the home language or one of the two home languages,
even though traditionally all schooling has been conducted in
English. We participated in an experiment wherein a random
selection of schools in the area were permitted to offer about
a third of the elementary curriculum in French and where a second sample of schools with children of comparable intelligence
scores and socioeconomic backgrounds served as a control or
comparison in that all their instruction was in English. After
a five-year run, the children in the "partial French" schools
clearly outperformed those in the control schools on tests in-
volving various aspects of *English* language skills and academic
content (such as math, learned partly via French) at the same
time as French had become for them a much more literate language (in contrast to mainly audio-lingual) because of the
reading and writing requirements of the French schooling. In
fact, recent reports show that the French-trained children are
consistently ahead of the control children in English-language
achievement test scores as well as in grade placement levels.
This means that they now have a much better chance to compete
with other American children in enterprises that call for educational abilities; they apparently have been lifted from the
typical low standing on scholastic achievement measures that
characterizes many ethnolinguistic groups in North America.

An important element in this transformation appears to be
a change in the self-views of the French-trained youngsters

who, our research has shown, begin to reflect a powerful pride
in being French, and a realization that their language is as
important a medium for education as English (Lambert, Giles, &
Picard, 1975). Similar community-based studies are underway
in the American Southwest, and these, too, are based on the belief that ethnolinguistic minorities need a strong educational
experience in their *own* languages and traditions before they
can cope in an "all-American" society or before they will *want*
to cope in such a society.

REFERENCES

Aellen, C., & Lambert, W.E. Ethnic identification and person-
    ality adjustments of Canadian adolescents of mixed Eng-
    lish-French parentage. *Canadian Journal of Behavioral
    Science,* 1969, *1*, 69-86.

Anisfeld, E. A comparison of the cognitive functioning of
    monolinguals and bilinguals. Unpublished Ph.D. disser-
    tation, McGill University, 1964.

Balkan, L. *Les effets du bilinguisme français-anglais sur
    les aptitudes intellectuelles.* Bruxelles: Aimav, 1970.

Ben-Zeev, S. The influence of bilingualism on cognitive
    development and cognitive strategy. Unpublished doctoral
    dissertation, University of Chicago, 1972.

Child, I.L. *Italian or American? The second generation in
    conflict.* New Haven: Yale University Press, 1943.

Cummins, J., & Gulutsan, M. Some effects of bilingualism
    on cognitive functioning. Mimeo. Edmonton, Alberta:
    University of Alberta, 1973.

Cummins, J. The influence of bilingualism on cognitive
    growth: A synthesis of research findings and explana-
    tory hypotheses. Mimeo. Dublin: St. Patrick's College,
    1976.

Dubé, N.C., & Herbert, G. St. John Valley Bilingual Edu-
    cation Project, prepared for the U.S. Department of
    Health, Education and Welfare under contract No. OEC-
    0-74-9331, August, 1975. Mimeo. (a).

Dubé, N.C., & Herbert, G. Evaluation of the St. John
    Valley Title VII Bilingual Education Program, 1970-1975,
    Madawaska, Maine, 1975. Mimeo. (b).

Gardner, R.C., & Lambert, W.E. *Attitudes and motivation in
    second-language learning.* Rowley, Mass.: Newbury House,
    1972.

Getzels, J.W., & Jackson, P.W. *Creativity and intelligence.*
    New York: Wiley, 1962.

Gordon, A.I. *Intermarriage.* Boston: Beacon Press, 1966.

Guilford, J.P. Creativity. *American Psychologist,* 1950, *5*,
    444-454.

Guilford, J.P. The structure of intellect. *Psychological Bulletin*, 1956, *53*, 267-293.

Ianco-Worrall, A.D. Bilingualism and cognitive development. *Child Development*, 1972, *43*, 1390-1400.

Lambert, W.E., & Anisfeld, E. A note on the relationship of bilingualism and intelligence. *Canadian Journal of Behavioral Science*, 1969, *1*, 123-128.

Lambert, W.E., Giles, H., & Albert, A. Language attitudes in a rural city in northern Maine. Mimeo. McGill University, 1974.

Lambert, W.E. A social psychology of bilingualism. *Journal of Social Issues*, 1967, *23*, 91-109.

Lambert, W.E., Giles, H., & Picard, O. Language attitudes in a French-American community. *International Journal of the Sociology of Language*, 1975, *4*, 127-152.

Lambert, W.E., & Tucker, G.R. *Bilingual education of children: The St. Lambert experiment.* Rowley, Mass.: Newbury House, 1972.

Leopold, W.F. *Speech development of a bilingual child* (4 vols.). Evanston, Illinois: Northwestern University Press, 1939-1949.

Long, K.K., & Padilla, A.M. Evidence for bilingual antecedents of academic success in a group of Spanish-American college students. Unpublished research report, Western Washington State College, 1970.

Padilla, A.M., & Long, K.K. An assessment of successful Spanish-American students at the University of New Mexico. Paper presented to the annual meeting of the AAAS, Rocky Mountain Division, Colorado Springs, 1969.

Park, R.E. Personality and cultural conflict. *Publication of the American Sociological Society*, 1931, *25*, 95-110. (Republished in R.E. Park, *Race and culture.* Glencoe, Illinois: The Free Press, 1964.)

Peal, E., & Lambert, W.E. The relation of bilingualism to intelligence. *Psychological Monographs*, 1962, *76*, 1-23.

Saucier, J.F. Psychiatric aspects of inter-ethnic marriages. Mimeo. McGill University, 1965.

Scott, S. The relation of divergent thinking to bilingualism: Cause or effect. Unpublished research report, McGill University, 1973.

Torrance, E.P., Gowan, J.C., Wu, J.M., & Aliotti, N.C. Creative functioning of monolingual and bilingual children in Singapore. *Journal of Educational Psychology*, 1970, *61*, 72-75.

Vygotsky, L.S. *Thought and language.* New York: M.I.T. Press, 1962.

Chapter 3

Mechanisms by Which Childhood
Bilingualism Affects Understanding
of Language and Cognitive Structures

SANDRA BEN-ZEEV

Bilingual Education Service Center

Research on the effects of bilingualism on cognition goes
at least as far back as the early 1900s. At that time the
question was formulated in terms of whether or not bilingualism affects performance on tests of general intelligence, and
the bulk of early studies, as reviewed by Arsenian (1932), concluded that intelligence is negatively affected by the presence
of bilingualism. However, as Lambert (Chapter 2 in this volume) has pointed out, these studies can largely be discounted
because of their failure to include the most basic controls.
In a review of later studies, Darcy (1953) concluded that bilinguals suffer from a language handicap when measured by verbal tests of intelligence but that there is no handicap on
tests of nonverbal intelligence.

In contrast to these conclusions regarding the relationship between bilingualism and intelligence, a positive relationship was found by Peal and Lambert (1962) in a study of
ten-year-old, middle-class, French-Canadian bilinguals. In
addition, this study revealed that the bilinguals were characterized by a more differentiated intelligence subtest profile
than their monolingual comparison group. This was a first
step toward determining more specifically what particular intellectual skills or processes bilingualism might affect. Because this study had not controlled for native intelligence,
however, its results could only be suggestive. Anisfeld (1964)
attempted to correct this by reanalyzing the original data to
eliminate subjects until groups could be matched for IQ. After this correction the results were somewhat attenuated but
still in the same direction. Anisfeld's report also included
other bilingual studies with a wider range of tests. Her find-

ings indicated superiority of bilinguals on intelligence sub-
tests of a kind which require "symbolic manipulation or mental
flexibility." She distinguished tests of this type from tests
of "creative flexibility." The latter tests were quite specific about requiring the subject to produce a variety of ideas
or types of response. The bilinguals were not found to be superior in this. When instructions do not specifically spell
out a requirement to be flexible, but are simply problem-solv-
ing oriented, the bilinguals tend to reflect a habit of taking
a flexible approach. Where instructions do set the subject to
be flexible, monolinguals respond the way the bilinguals do
and group differences disappear. By this interpretation the
response characteristics of bilinguals are a matter of response
set rather than basic ability difference.

Torrance (1970) predicted that bilinguals would perform
more poorly on both tests of ideational fluency (number of ideas produced) and "creative flexibility" (number of distinctly
different ideas produced). His study of Chinese and Malayan
children whose second language was English confirmed this.
Torrance's negative predictions were based on assumptions concerning effects of associative interference between the words
of the two languages on associative fluency and recall.

Speculation about such negative effects of interlingual
interference on thought processes as well as possible positive
effects has a long history. As early as 1919, Stern maintained that

> The difference in language...not only leads to the asso-
> ciated phenomenon of interference, but is a powerful
> stimulus to individual acts of thought, to comparisons
> and differentiations, to the realization of the scopes
> and limitation of concepts, to the understanding of
> nice shades of meaning (Stern, 1919, p. 107).

Stern recognizes, in this statement, that bilingualism
can have both negative and positive effects. The negative effect would be "interference" and the positive effect would be
a "stimulus to individual acts of thought." The thesis of this
chapter is that these are not two separate effects but that it
is the "interference" which is the stimulus to "individual
acts of thought."

The remainder of this chapter includes further evidence
for the effects of interlingual interference on the thought
processes of bilinguals. The emphasis is not on interlingual
interference per se, however, but on the cognitive consequences
of the strategies or processes which develop in the bilingual
child as he struggles to overcome interlingual interference
operating on the structural level of language.

Four different mechanisms are proposed to describe the
means by which the bilingual child attempts to resolve the in-

terference between his languages. These mechanisms are not intended to be definitive and they are subject to revision with
further evidence. They are the result of extrapolations from
and interpretations of the data which now exist. The assumption behind all four mechanisms is that the primary effect of
bilingualism is on language-learning strategies, and that it
is through this channel that bilingualism may affect general
thought processes. These mechanisms all involve resolving interference at the structural level of language. They are as
follows: (1) *language analysis;* (2) *sensitivity to feedback
cues* indicating correctness or incorrectness of present language orientation; (3) *maximization of structural differences
between languages;* (4) *neutralization of structure within a
language.*

The first two mechanisms are especially important because
of their potentially positive effects on symbolic processing
in general. Evidence for such effects is included in the discussion of each of these two mechanisms. The other two mechanisms may also have more generalizing effects but these are
harder to predict and have not yet been investigated.

For mechanisms 1, 3, and 4 the content on which the strategy is focused is clearly the structure of language itself,
primarily at the syntactic level, though not excluding the
possibility of involvement with other aspects of language
structure. Mechanism 2 concerns language structure also but
at a more superficial level, and this mechanism concerns cues
from the environment which are associated with language in addition to cues from language structure itself.

Knowledge of how language structure is acquired by monolingual children is still developing and knowledge of how bilinguals learn language structure has just begun. As more
evidence accumulates in these areas, the efficiency of the proposed mechanisms as useful ways of organizing the data will
become clearer.

LANGUAGE ANALYSIS

The hypothesis here is that the bilingual child sometimes
resolves the interference between his languages by means of
awareness of the two different ways in which his languages
process a given paradigm.

This sort of process can be observed in some of the "interlanguage" errors which children make as they acquire a second language. The following example (Selinker, Swain, & Dumas,
1975) is from an English-speaking seven-year-old learning
French in a special school immersion program:

> *Un jour qui chaud.*   (Correct English: *A hot day.*)
>   (Correct French: *Un jour chaud.*)

In this example the child has used the correct French order of noun and modifying adjective while at the same time adhering partway to the English rule that if the modifying adjective follows its noun it can only do so as part of a relative clause (e.g., *A day that is hot.*) The attempt to combine the two paradigms is an indication of an awareness of both of them at some level.

Another example of the same type is reported by Ravem (1968). Correct use of the *do* auxiliary in English requires abstract deep structure processing because this form has no semantic correlate and serves strictly structural purposes (Ervin-Tripp, 1971). In Norwegian there is no auxiliary verb *do*. Also, in the case of negative sentences in Norwegian there is a different placement rule for main verbs than for verbs with auxiliaries. The negative follows the main verb when it is alone but precedes the verb when it is with an auxiliary. The English sentence *I don't like that* would be translated into Norwegian as *I like not that*. Since *do* is not in the Norwegian language the Norwegian sentence has no auxiliary in this case. Therefore the negative follows the verb.

Ravem's six-year-old Norwegian child who was learning English used a form that corresponded neither to the Norwegian form nor to the English form. The form he used was *I not like that*. Superficially this sounds like an early stage in the development of the English negative (Klima & Bellugi, 1966); it cannot be that, however, because this child is already capable of forming auxiliaries, which children in that early developmental stage are not. The sentence form which was used by the child implies his understanding that the sentence does require an auxiliary verb in English, even if he is not capable of rendering the particular modal *do* yet. If he did not recognize this then he would not have placed the negative element before the main verb; he would have placed it after the verb as in Norwegian.

Evidence that bilinguals may analyze language more intensively than monolinguals comes from three studies, Ben-Zeev's study of Hebrew-English bilingual children from families in professional occupations (1972), her study of Spanish-English bilingual children of low-socioeconomic class (1975), and Worrall's (1970; also Ianco-Worrall, 1972) study of Afrikaans-English bilinguals in South Africa, presumably middle-class. In all these studies the bilingual group and its monolingual control groups were equated for age, sex, social class, and intelligence. In the Ben-Zeev studies ethnicity was the same for both groups, and this seems to have been true for the Worrall (now Ianco-Worrall) study also. In these studies the age range was four years to nine years of age. Worrall's study had 30 subjects, Ben-Zeev's had 98 and 188 subjects, respectively.

Worrall's bilingual sample was limited to bilinguals whose parents each consistently spoke a different language to the child. Selection was determined by ability to pass a test of basic verbal skills in both languages. Ben-Zeev's criterion for selection was performance on a translation test in which the child must translate sentences in each language into the other language, where word-for-word translation was impossible.

The Afrikaans-English study and the Hebrew-English study both found evidence that bilinguals are capable at an earlier age than other children of separating the meaning of a word from its sound. Group differences of this sort were not found in the Spanish-English study. Presumably this ability is the result of learning that the words of the two languages are characterized by different sound representations for a given idea. This does not indicate language analysis in a direct way but it does indicate achievement of a preliminary stage in which the child understands that a sound representation is not the same as the idea which it represents. This frees representations for later more abstract structural analysis.

In Ianco-Worrall's study the bilingual children excelled not in active analysis of representations but in ability to state the principle that names are arbitrarily assigned to things. Ben-Zeev's Hebrew-English bilinguals were superior to their comparison group in ability to play with words, which is nearer to what might be expected as the result of increased analysis of language. For example, these bilinguals excelled on the following item:

> This is named *plane*, right? (Experimenter holds up
> toy airplane)
> In this game its name is *turtle* . . . .
> *Can the turtle fly?* (Correct answer: *Yes*.)
> How does the "turtle" fly? (Correct answer: *With
> its wings*.)

The reason why the Spanish-English bilinguals did not show superiority in performing this type of task may be related to the lower socioeconomic level of this sample, which included many families on public assistance. Opportunity for language experience and the interest in language which come with high educational level of the family may be an important factor in interaction with bilingualism. Pride in being bilingual may also be an important factor. The one-language one-parent home situation of the Afrikaans-English bilinguals was probably often a self-conscious plan by the parents to foster bilingualism in the child. The Hebrew-English bilinguals' parents sent them to Hebrew day school even though the children were bilingual anyway, which indicates an attempt to foster the bilingualism. For the Spanish-English bilingual children pride was

less evident. When asked which language they spoke better they
usually said Spanish, but when asked which language they liked
better they usually said English. Also, being in public
schools in large city neighborhoods, they were relatively more
exposed to the intolerance of foreign language often found in
the United States.

In the Hebrew-English study there was more direct evidence
for better ability to analyze language on the part of the bilinguals. The later items of the word substitution test required much more than simple substitution of one word for another meaningful word as in the preceding example. They required violation of selectional restrictions. For example, the
following item requires violation of the rule that a mass noun
takes a singular verb:

> For this game the way we say *they* is to say *spaghetti*.
> How do we say: *They are good children?*
> (Correct answer: *Spaghetti are good children.*)
> What do we mean when we say *spaghetti?* (Correct answer:
> *They.*)

The most difficult test item requires violation of strict
subcategorization rules. That is, the subject is required to
replace one part of speech by another which it cannot normally
replace. In this case the task is especially difficult because the word which must be inserted in place of the original
word in the sentence is also more semantically meaningful and
tends to carry all its connotations with it, which leads to
mistakes:

> For this game the way we say *in* or *into* is to say the
> word *clean* . . . . *See this doll? See this house?*
> *Tell me where the doll is going* (experimenter pushes
> doll inside of house).
> (Correct answer: *The doll is going clean the house.*)
> Does the dollhouse get cleaner, dirtier, or does it
> stay the same when the doll does that?
> (Correct answer: *It stays the same.*)

The Hebrew-English bilinguals were significantly superior
on this task to their monolingual control groups from equally
well educated families. For the Spanish-English bilinguals
there were no group trends on this item. However, when types
of errors were analyzed it was found that in comparison to
their monolingual (English) control group the Spanish-English
bilinguals made significantly fewer errors of a global, primitive type. In this type of error the child is satisfied to
simply utter the substitute word in place of the entire sentence. For example, instead of saying "Spaghetti are good

children" the child merely says "Spaghetti." He is unable to treat the sentence analytically.

Ability to treat sentence structure analytically and with playful flexibility as in the symbol substitution task does not imply superiority in ordinary grammar rule usage. In neither study were the bilinguals superior in tests of understanding of ordinary grammar. The Hebrew-English study included a test of ability to generalize ordinary phrase structure rules, adapted from Berko (1958). Example:

> *This is a lod. Here is another lod. What are these?*
> (Experimenter points to two of them.)   (Correct
> answer: *lods*.)

The test covered a broader range of structures than Berko's to correspond to the greater age range of the subjects.

For the Spanish-English study, samples of the child's storytelling were taken and analyzed for grammatical mistakes. The bilinguals made significantly more mistakes on all measures. Their sentences, however, were as complex as those of the monolinguals, as measured by percentage of clausal sentences.

The superiority of the bilinguals on the symbol substitution task can also be contrasted with their vocabulary performance. Both the Hebrew-English bilinguals and the Spanish-English bilinguals were very significantly inferior in performance on the Peabody Picture Vocabulary Test as compared to their respective monolingual control groups. This in itself is not surprising. Having to share their language experience between two languages, the bilinguals have less opportunity for experience with the vocabulary of either. Presumably with increasing age and experience the deficit will become less marked. The relative lack of experience with each language probably has some limiting effect on knowledge of standard grammatical rules within each language as well as on vocabulary, although the grammar limitation should be less serious because repetitiveness and redundancy in grammar compensate for inexperience. Symbol substitution, on the other hand, depends not on mastery of particular words or particular production rules but on a grasp of the basic idea that the structure of a language is different from the phonological representations and meaningful words in which it is embodied, and that it is arbitrary and subject to change, rather than immutable or in the nature of things. The experience that bilinguals have in learning two different language structures apparently fosters this kind of consciousness. Bilinguals were better able to analyze language as an abstract system, particularly the Hebrew-English middle-class bilinguals.

Other tests in the two Ben-Zeev studies consisted of non-verbal material but were also intended to test structural un-

derstanding. It was presumed that if the bilinguals perform
differently from monolinguals on these tests it is as a result
of generalization from system analysis skills developed in language-learning efforts.

The Spanish-English sample was given two somewhat different tests of ability to classify and reclassify. Each required the subject to classify items consistently, to switch to
another type of classification of the same items, and then
switch to still a third type of classification. One test was
based on Inhelder & Piaget (1964, Chapter Seven, part 2). The
other required a reversal shift and required the ability to resist fitting together the stimuli into a global whole. The bilinguals performed better on both parts of the test.

On a test of matrix transposition (Bruner & Kenney, 1966)
the Hebrew-English bilinguals were better able to name the underlying dimensions in the task. The same trend was shown for
the Spanish-English bilinguals. The bilinguals were especially good on an item which required the child to demonstrate or
describe how two items in the matrix which differ in one basic
dimension but are similar in the other basic dimension are
"the same."

Subjects in the Hebrew-English study were also given the
Raven's Matrices Test. There were no group differences in total score; however, the bilinguals were better able to resist
the error of simply choosing the response item closest to the
choice point instead of scanning the whole field of possible
responses. They appeared to be approaching the task with a
more analytic strategy.

Another test which was included in both the Hebrew-English and the Spanish-English studies is of a verbal type and
is concerned with word association. Interest is in whether
the child responds to a meaningful stimulus word with a response word which could follow the stimulus word in a sentence
sequence. Responses of the same form class (called paradigmatic responses) have been found to increase in frequency with
age. An early explanation for this is that with increasing age
there is increased opportunity to experience each particular
word in many different verbal contexts, making the child more
likely to abstract that aspect of the word which is constant
through all its various contexts of usage, hence to abstract
its form class membership (Ervin, 1961a, 1963; Jenkins & Palermo, 1964). More recently it has been suggested (Clifton, 1967;
McNeill, 1971) that so-called paradigmatic responses are based
on concept relationships of the stimulus word and represent
placement of the word within a semantic feature system in memory storage.

If the earlier interpretation is correct then one would
expect bilinguals to have fewer responses of the paradigmatic
type than would other children because bilinguals must divide

their time between languages and thus have less experience with particular words. The lower vocabulary scores found for bilinguals bears out this experiential deficit.

However, if paradigmatic responses are based on development of a semantic feature system a deficit for bilinguals is not as clearly predictable, even though the low vocabulary of the bilinguals can still be expected to be a disadvantage. What little evidence there is, is against the idea that bilinguals have reduced attention to semantics. Ianco-Worrall (1972) asked subjects to judge which of two words is more similar to a standard word, a word similar to the standard in meaning or a word similar in sound. The bilinguals were more likely to judge as similar the word similar in meaning to the standard word.

The results for both bilingual studies were quite similar although the implications are not completely clear. Both sets of bilinguals tended to have more paradigmatic responses but in neither case were the differences significant. In both studies also the latency of paradigmatic responses in particular was higher for the bilinguals, significantly so in the Hebrew-English study. The bilinguals also in both cases gave more responses which showed task difficulty, such as unrelated responses and clang sound responses. Much of the difficulty of this task for the bilinguals is explainable by their low vocabulary, since vocabulary was highly and positively correlated to paradigmatic responses on this test.

It seems that although the bilinguals lack the lexical knowledge to make notable use of an internal semantic feature system on the word association task, they do seem to be making efforts in this direction, as reflected in the longer latency for paradigmatic responses. Ordinarily one would expect that for persons with limited vocabulary it would be easier to resort to a sequential response characteristic of younger children than to attempt the more demanding paradigmatic type of response (e.g., *Cut-Paper* or *Cut-Something* versus *Cut-Snip* or *Cut-Paste* or *Cut-Stop*). Sequential responses can make use of sequential probabilities but more importantly they allow the child to place the stimulus word in a situational framework, which relieves the challenge to enter into a semantic feature system. Bilinguals do not resort to frequent situational responses to offset their poor vocabulary. There are no group differences for sequential responses. In fact, there is some evidence that bilinguals resort less to situational responses. In the Spanish-English study it was very difficult to get the younger children to give one-word responses. They tended to root the stimulus word to a concrete situation by giving multi-word responses of the following type: *Cut — I never gonna cut your hair*, or *When — When you do something*. It is interesting that in spite of the low vocabulary of the younger Spanish-English bilinguals they tended to give *fewer* of the multiword situational responses than their monolingual counterparts.

In summary of this section, the three bilingual studies reviewed have provided considerable evidence for the existence of an analytic strategy toward language on the part of bilingual children and some evidence for the generalization of this strategy to other kinds of structures.

SENSITIVITY TO FEEDBACK CUES

Sensitivity to feedback cues is a strategy presumed to involve active scanning efforts to spot cues indicating correctness or incorrectness of present language orientation which then trigger reorganization efforts. The cues may come from aspects of language structure, although from relatively superficial details of structure, or they may come from details of the environmental situation. Many kinds of cues are relevant, including syntactic and phonetic linguistic cues, and aspects of the environmental setting such as type of interlocutor, place, topic. Reactions of interlocutors may also become important cues, and the child may become especially sensitive to emotional reactions.

The motivation for this strategy is conceived to be both cognitive and emotional. Considering first the cognitive, it is necessary to assume, for this strategy, that the ability to keep languages apart cannot be completely accomplished by a simple on-off switching mechanism. An earlier theory (Penfield and Roberts, 1959) proposed that the neurological systems underlying the two languages of bilinguals are functionally separate in such a way that when one is on the other must be off. This theory implies that linguistic interference does not occur. However, a study by Preston (1965) invalidated the Penfield and Roberts theory. Using the Stroop Color-Word Test this study found that when the subject sets himself to respond in one language interference from stimuli in the other language does occur. In reviewing Preston's study, Macnamara (1967a, p. 67) concluded the need for a two-switch model:

A bilingual can decide to speak in one language rather than the other independent of his environment, and so he acts as though he had a language switch controlling his language output system. On the other hand, when he sees some print or hears some words in one of his languages he automatically carries out the decoding process in the appropriate language. In this case he acts as though he had a language switch at the beginning of his input or decoding system which is controlled by the environment.

However, Macnamara's formulation of an automatic two-switch model is still too simple. Kolers (1966) has shown that switching takes time and therefore special processing, and therefore it is not simply automatic. Kolers found that although comprehension of linguistically mixed passages was not inferior to that of unilingual ones, speeds for reading and spontaneous production were very much slower. A somewhat different study by Macnamara (1967b) had similar results.

Since switching is difficult, it would be useful for the child to develop special monitoring processes which pick up cues to warn him when switching will be required. And since the child must not only be ready to switch when required but also be able to resist interference and to remain within the structure of one language, the bilingual child may be especially sensitive both to cues indicating the need to reorganize and switch to the other language structure and to cues indicating successful preservation of a given framework.

The extent of monitoring may depend in part on the degree of unpredictability he experiences in his language environment. The less predictable is a language by interlocutor, place, topic, etc., the more sensitive will the child need to be to capture whatever cues exist. The extent of monitoring may also depend upon the extent to which the environment demands frequent internal reorganization, as when the child is frequently required to translate for others in his environment or, as in the case of Worrall's subjects, who when conversing with both parents simultaneously would have to speak a different language to each, which necessitates continual language switching.

No matter what the conditions of bilingual language learning, it seems to be cognitively more difficult to become bilingual than to become monolingual. Parents often report that their children who are exposed to two languages avoid the problem by refusing to speak one of the languages. It seems that only when the status of the two languages is both high and relatively equal, and when both languages are spoken by individuals important to the child that the child rises to the challenge of becoming bilingual. Children who become bilingual early do so in response to environmental demands, otherwise the language with less status does not develop far. (For the contrary view that bilingualism requires no extra effort, on the assumption that language acquisition is primarily innate, see Lenneberg, 1967; McNeill, 1966.)

Bilingual children seem to be required to exercise extra effort in language learning. They may be disposed to attend to feedback cues as the most immediate way of accommodating to the immediate language requirements.

As for emotional forces which may foster sensitivity to feedback, the bilingual child is in a situation of uncertainty. He is likely to make mistakes by interpreting stimuli from one language as belonging to the other, by speaking one language when the other is required, and by outright interlingual interference in his own speech. He is subject to confusion and often also to ridicule, the extent of ridicule depending on the degree of acceptance of both of his languages by his larger environment and the degree of acceptance he finds for his language mistakes. Anxiety over confusion and ridicule may be a strong motivation for development of sensitivity to perceptual feedback cues pertaining to language.

Evidence for this strategy comes from the Ben-Zeev (1975) Spanish-English study, which included several different measures to test sensitivity to cues. The test of classification and reclassification in this study provided that whenever a subject perseverated by giving the same classification twice instead of switching to another classification the experimenter would present special hints in the next trial which pointed to the need to reclassify. Thus if the child was stuck on classifying by shape, round and square, the hint set would also include triangles, which made it difficult to classify by shape again into two groups. The bilinguals were significantly better able to use these hints as cues to successful restructuring.

The bilinguals scored significantly higher on the Wechsler Intelligence Scale for Children Picture Completion subtest. This was presumably because they engaged in more scanning of the details of the presented picture to check how it deviated from their internal model of what such a picture ought to include.

An unanticipated characteristic appearing in the aforementioned classification test which is relevant to the hypothesis of sensitivity to cues on the part of bilinguals was the unusual attention to details of classification which they showed. On the classification task the bilinguals would classify the objects into two consistent classes, as directed, but they would then tend to make gratuitous subclassifications within the two major classes. This in itself had no effect on the correctness of their responses, which depended only on ability to make the major classifications. However, the result of this behavior was a slight tendency to disorientation, because occasionally they would lose track of the levels involved and describe their classification in terms of the subclasses instead of the major division. This sort of elaboration of structural detail was more characteristic of the older bilinguals (seven to nine years of age). In Torrance's study (1970) a tendency toward elaboration was similarly noted for bilinguals.

A concern with major details was evident in a test in which the subject had to tell the experimenter the story shown in a sequence of cartoon pictures. The bilinguals more often noticed and included in their stories a necessary detail which

integrated the parts of the picture sequence better. This finding is relevant to the analytic strategy discussed earlier, but
it also seems relevant here.

The results described in the preceding paragraphs are explainable by attention to cognitive cues, but the following result seems to depend upon affective sensitivity as well. On a
test designed to measure the level of egocentrism the bilinguals were more reactive to the standard neutral probes given
by the experimenter. The probes reduced the level of egocentrism more for the bilinguals than for the other children. It
is as if the bilinguals were more apt to interpret the probe as
a hint to look for mistakes, as if they were more open to correction and guidance.

Procedures such as these should be carried out with other
sets of bilinguals from other ethnic groups. These particular
subjects were mostly Mexican, and one cannot be sure whether
or not the result was fostered by a particular Mexican social
sensitivity. Both the bilingual and monolingual groups were
mostly Mexican in origin, but the bilinguals were from less
assimilated families with a stronger sense of traditional values (as shown by parent questionnaire data). The finding by
Genesee, Tucker, and Lambert (1975) that English-speaking children in French school immersion programs are more sensitive to
the communication requirements of blindfolded listeners than
are other children gives support to the generality of greater
social sensitivity for children who speak two languages.

Evidence for attention of the bilinguals to cues from language structure came from a test called Verbal Transformations
(Warren & Warren, 1966), which was used in both Ben-Zeev studies. In this test a nonsense word is repeated continuously by
means of a tape loop and the subject must report what he hears.
It has been established that at about age six children begin
to be susceptible to the illusion that adults have on this test,
namely, that the verbal stimulus is repeatedly changing. In
both Ben-Zeev studies the bilinguals were found to be significantly more susceptible to this illusion than the monolinguals,
perceiving more changes and more different types of words.

In the procedure just described the continuous quality of
the verbal stimulus leads the hearer to expect ordinary speech.
The perception of changes in the verbal stimulus is probably
the result of processing effort in the attempt to make sense
out of the stimulus. The fact that the bilinguals perceive a
high number of auditory changes represents increased processing effort on their part to achieve auditory reorganization in
response to feedback indicating absence of acceptable closure.

However, when asked afterwards whether the changes they
reported were "real" or not, the bilinguals did tend to confirm
that there had been changes more often than did the monolinguals but the difference between groups was not significant.

If we regard the experimenter's question concerning whether the changes are real as a cue which directs the child's attention to possible alternative interpretations, then perhaps this is another instance of the bilinguals' readiness to respond to the alternatives implicit in cues, as in the perceptual "hints" on the classification test, and especially as in the response to "suggestions" from the experimenter on the egocentrism probe.

The latter finding may suggest that the bilinguals' reports of greater changes of the Verbal Transformations Test may have been a simple response phenomenon to please the experimenter rather than a perceptual phenomenon. However, certain controls provided in the test make it likely that the bilinguals did actually perceive more changes. For one thing, they perceived more changes on the stimulus that was clearer than the stimulus that was relatively vague, as did the monolinguals; for another, the changes they heard were as phonemically similar to those of the actual stimulus as those heard by the monolinguals. Certain children reported changes deviating widely from the stimulus and from each other, which leads to suspicion of "intentional" changes, but the bilinguals did not do this more than others.

In general, the kinds of cues to which bilinguals were more sensitive were of various types, including details of structure, perceptual indications of error, and particular interpersonal cues.

MAXIMIZATION OF STRUCTURAL DIFFERENCES BETWEEN LANGUAGES

It is proposed that one of the mechanisms used by bilinguals to keep their languages from mutual interference is to maximize the differences between them by overgeneralizing the regularity and superparadigmatic consistency of rules *within* each language in cases where these rules differ *between* languages.

Selinker, Swain, and Dumas (1975) list a number of strategies which they have found in children learning a second language in a school immersion program. One of these strategies is overgeneralization. Their example fits the mechanism proposed here because the child is overgeneralizing a rule from the second language, in this case, French, which is in contrast to the rules of his initial language, English: *une maison nouvelle*. The correct order in this particular case should be *une nouvelle maison,* which happens to be the same order as the English translation, *a new house*. What the child did in this case was to base the order on the usual rule in French that the adjective follows the noun it modifies, even though it does not apply in this particular case. The suggestion here is that the child was attempting to maximize the contrast between the typical French and the typical English forms.

Selinker *et al.* also describe transfer as another strategy used by second-language learners. Example: *Ça regarde très drôle,* by transfer from English, *It looks very funny,* instead of the correct *Ça semble très drôle.* If we define "strategy" as an operating perceptual or production set used by the child, then it seems as though transfer is more a matter of lack of differentiation between languages associated with a low level of bilingualism than an actual strategy for language learning. Learning to become bilingual involves learning to recognize one's tendencies to naive transfer because this is one of the kinds of interference which the child must overcome. Overgeneralization, on the other hand, seems more likely to become a positive strategy because it can serve as a mechanism to emphasize the structural distinction between languages and thus to keep them apart.

Ervin-Tripp (1973) has shown that early rules of language structure are grasped by means of the saliency of the particular rule. Saliency can be a matter of the variety of types employing the same contrast. In reference to the acquisition of the regular past tense rule in English, for example, the child is enabled to grasp the rule because a great many different verbs all form the past tense with the same (-d, -t, -ed) morpheme.

Rule perception must be more difficult in the case of children learning two languages simultaneously. The regular past tense rule is not the same in one language as in the other, so any underlying constancy of pattern is more difficult to discover. Swain's data (1972a) indicate that the period of acquisition of early rules is longer for bilingual than for monolingual children. She also points out that "we cannot talk about interference in child bilingualism until after the period of differentiation. That is to say, differentiation is logically prior to intrusion."

The child cannot understand his two languages as distinct systems until he has grasped a number of basic structural rules. Initially the child learning both languages simultaneously applies a given rule in all contexts, indicating that the systems have not yet been differentiated (Swain, 1972a, 1972b). Once the child has sufficient data to grasp that he has two separate systems, certain records of bilingual children (Burling, 1959; Ronjat, 1913), indicate a very active effort to distinguish the two contexts and to find translation equivalents. Before this the stage of naive rule generalization prevails in which the two languages have not yet been differentiated. This comes in the wake of the earliest language-learning period in which the bilingual finds it unusually difficult to make any rule generalizations because of the overwhelming variation of forms corresponding to any rule. At that point the child has no means

yet to separate the way a given rule is contrastingly formulated in each language.

It may be that the very difficulty which the bilingual
child experiences in formulating the earliest rules creates in
him greater pressure toward generalization. Once he has begun
to understand that he has two different language systems he may
apply this readiness to generalize by using it to extend and
integrate the various rules within each language as a way of
distinguishing between languages. In some cases this may lead
to unwarranted overgeneralization within each language, making
the language seem more consistent than it is. In other respects it may contribute to an unusually deep understanding of
language structure.

Greenfield (1971) found that perceptual notions such as
squareness are learned better by young children if the children are made to perform many actions in relation to objects
exhibiting that trait. However, once the child has learned a
term describing a related attribute, e.g., "round," then whether or not the child was subjected to different physical encounters with objects exhibiting that trait no longer mattered.
At that point in learning, exposure to the contrasting labels
"round" and "square" became more effective in learning to understand squareness than associating the word "square" with a
variety of activities.

It is possible that the need for variation which is essential for discrimination of meaning at some point becomes
shifted from the perceptual to the verbal plane, so that after
the child has reached a certain basic comprehension of vocabulary and structure, then the more varied the verbal activity
and verbal contexts in which the item appears, the deeper and
more complex is the understanding of the item.

For the bilingual child the fact that a given concept may
be associated with two different universes of discourse in the
different languages may create in him a deeper understanding
of that concept. He may come to see also that a given aspect
of the referent situation is represented two different ways in
the structures of his languages and that each of these forms of
representation is consistent with other rules within each of
the respective language systems. This may suggest to the child
a way to keep his languages from interfering with each other.
If he can learn how the various rules within one language are
consistent with each other he can understand how each language
constitutes a *system* of rules. He can then make use of the
rule redundancies within a language system as cues to maintaining his own speech within one system and as a means for pre-
venting interlingual interference.

The strategy of overgeneralization of rules within one
language, as described by Selinker *et al*. (1975), can be taken
as an indication that the child is trying to view each of his

languages as a consistent system and to maximize the difference
between his two language systems.

The hypothesis here, to repeat, is that bilinguals become
aware of their languages as internally consistent systems more
than do other children because this kind of understanding provides a way of separating their languages from each other.
This hypothesis is the most speculative of those discussed in
this chapter, yet there are some hints in the literature that
it is at least worthwhile formulating it as a basis for future
research.

As pointed out by Dale (1976, p. 215), Jakobson had earlier claimed that children learn the phonemes of their language
through a process of acquiring one distinctive feature contrast
at a time, each contrast being added to the language in a unified, complete fashion. Yet studies have found that the presence of a contrast in a single pair of phonemes does not guar-
antee that the contrast will be used elsewhere. For example,
the child Mackie (Moskowitz, 1970) had mastered the voiced-
voiceless contrast in the phoneme pairs /p/-/b/ and /t/-/d/.
He had also mastered the stop-fricative contrast in the pairs
/p/-/f/ and /t/-/s/, as well as the labial-dental contrast in
another set of pairs. These three types of contrast are sufficient to specify the six basic fricatives of English: /f/,
/v/, /s/, /z/, /θ/, and /ð/. Yet Mackie had mastered only two
fricatives: /f/ and /s/. This indicates that once learned a
feature does not necessarily spread rapidly throughout the
system to all relevant segments.

On the other hand, Burling (1959) reported that his son
Stephen acquired the voiced-voiceless contrast and almost immediately expanded his set of stops from three to six. It may
be more than coincidence that Stephen was highly bilingual.
One example can only be suggestive, but the possibility is in-
triguing.

On the phonemic level, as on the syntactic and other levels of language, grasp of a language rule in one situation does
not automatically extend to grasp of the same rule in other
contexts. Perhaps bilingual children are more ready to extend
the application of a rule to its various contexts than are other children because of the need to see each of his languages
as consistent. The consequences of this readiness to generalize are not all positive. According to Bellugi (1968) ordinary language learning proceeds by increasing understanding of
the conditions on rules. The bilinguals might grasp general
rules and extend them more quickly but by the same token they
may be slower in attending to the increasingly detailed modifications of rules within the language as they conflict with other rules of the language.

The bilinguals would excel in those areas of language
where there is superparadigmatic consistency among various

rules or integration of various rules into a larger whole. The distinctive feature system on the phoneme level is one example of this type of subsystem. Most aspects of language are not as clearly ordered as this, and usually in a living language there are many inconsistencies between rules within the general system. Greenberg (1957, 1963) has described another aspect of language which tends toward a larger consistency. He describes a tendency for a language to be consistent through various paradigms in respect to the order of appearance of topic in relation to comment. For example, if the noun appears before the adjective in a particular language, then topic is likely to come before comment in other paradigms which belong to the language as well. Thus noun should precede genitive, subject should precede verb. If the present hypothesis is correct, then here again bilinguals can be expected to learn the consistent order system of a language faster than do other children. The more a language can be reduced to consistent rules, the more easily can it be separated from the other language if the corresponding rule system of the other language is different.

NEUTRALIZATION OF STRUCTURE

The various mechanisms described in this chapter are mechanisms aimed at counteracting structural interference. The general hypothesis for all the mechanisms is that bilinguals try to maintain the structural independence of their two languages as systems. This particular section proposes the existence of a process which helps prevent structural interference for some particular aspect of structure which is formed differently between languages by simplifying structure *within* one of the languages. The proposed process will be called here "neutralization."

Certain studies have found that the speech of some bilingual children is relatively unmarked in structure, as if language development was in their case retarded and relatively undifferentiated. Considering the very difficult language-learning task which confronts bilinguals, it would not be surprising if this were true. Yet it is hypothesized here that in many cases structural simplification, including relative absence of marking, is the result of a positive strategy which has as its purpose the prevention of interference between languages by means of temporarily neutralizing the structure of one of the languages at a point of conflict.

That simplification can be a useful strategy is seen in the practice of older bilinguals as they switch from one language to another or as they insert a concept word from one language into the general structural framework of the other language. Pfaff's (1976) protocols of Spanish-English bilinguals switching languages in informal conversation with each other show the following: When the switch into English begins with a verb, the speaker regularly presents the English verb in the form of an infinitive or present participle. These latter forms are characterized by structural neutrality, since they do not require inflection for tense, person, or gender, as any other verb form would. This verb neutrality does not result in structural ambiguity, however, because the obligatory inflections are expressed by a Spanish auxiliary or by another Spanish main verb in the sentence. In effect, a clash of structures has been prevented by means of rearrangement of the way in which obligatory inflectional categories are expressed in the sentence.

In Pfaff's examples it is interesting that many of the modifications of the Spanish structure occur *before* the point of switch into English. This indicates that the switch could not have been the result of a sudden whim in the middle of the sentence and that the switch had to be planned for before the sentence began, indicating the presence of forethought and flexibility of approach:

Male adolescent speaker:
Bueno, porqué te hicieron beat up ése?
'Well, why did they beat you up, man?'

Same speaker, after receiving reply:
Y nomas por ése te catiaron?
'And just for that they beat you up?'

Notice that the second sentence, in which there was no language switch, required only one verb to express the action of beating up. We can infer that the reason why the same concept required two verbs for its expression in the sentence containing the language switch was so that the prior verb in Spanish could carry the obligatory inflections, which have been neutralized in the English insertion.

Speaker:
Tu lo underestimate a Chito.
'You underestimate Chito.'

In the above sentence the presence of the subject word "tu" anticipates the switch into English in the verb which follows. In informal conversation the pronoun subject is usually deleted because it is redundant with the verb inflection which follows. In this case the speaker anticipates and plans for the absence of inflection on the neutralized English verb by compensating for it through inclusion of the pronoun subject.

The preceding examples are from older speakers with developed language skills, but does neutralization as a positive strategy also occur for children? Evidence for a similar process can be derived from errors made by seven-year-old English speakers beginning to learn French in a school language immersion program (Selinker *et al.*, 1975). These children often used the infinitive instead of the properly inflected third person form of the verb. ("Quand on *faire* 'wouf,' il entend," instead of the correct, "Quand on fait 'wouf,' il entend." When we go "wouf," he listens.)

Why does the child use the infinitive form of the verb in cases such as these? The infinitive is not correct in this case in either of the child's languages, so its use cannot be merely a matter of transfer. It is not a type of mistake typical of monolingual speakers of either language. Its presence must be the result of the implicit confrontation between the two languages. The presence of the infinitive seems to be an interlanguage phenomenon, a kind of compromise. The child has not yet mastered the correct form of the verb for his second language, yet he is aware that he cannot merely insert the type of verb inflection typical of his first language in this context. The compromise solution is to use the infinitive, which is neutral in inflection and does not violate the structure of either language, even though it is not correct in either language.

In cases where English is the language which is the less well known of the bilingual's two languages it is especially difficult to tell whether a particular mistake is the result of an active neutralization process or something else, because of the relative paucity of inflection in English structure. Studies of the English speech of Spanish-English bilingual children of school age show irregularities in the grammar of these children as compared to children of the same age, social class, and ethnic background who are not bilingual (Ben-Zeev, 1975; Politzer & Ramirez, 1973), but it is difficult to tell the reason. A prominent tendency found in both studies was for verbs to appear unmarked by inflection, at least intermittently (e.g., "He *see* the snowman."). The reason could be delayed language development, and indeed, this speech seems similar in some ways to the "telegraphic" speech characteristic of an early stage of monolingual language development. It also resembles pidgin speech. Yet it is different from pidgin in that the bilingual speech is quite variable, sometimes leaving the verb unmarked and sometimes expressing the inflections, even for the same child using the same verb. It could also represent transfer from the Spanish, since the third person singular in Spanish is unmarked, just as in the preceding example. Yet transfer is unlikely to be the explanation, since the same unmarked form is used also for past tense ("Yesterday he *see* the

snowman."), whereas the Spanish third person does mark the past
tense third person singular.

The same simplification process used by the children discussed previously who were learning French may be functioning
here also. It is impossible to tell for certain, since in English the infinitive and the unmarked form of the verb are the
same. The Spanish-English bilinguals may be intending the neutral infinitive also. More work remains to be done to estab-
lish whether a positive strategy of neutralization does exist
and in what circumstances it may occur.

INTERLINGUAL INTERFERENCE AND LANGUAGE CONVERGENCE

Interference between languages does, of course, occur repeatedly, in spite of the various mechanisms to counteract it
which have been discussed in this chapter. The result may be
some degree of language convergence, most often at the semantic
level. Syntax is far more resistant to convergence or fusion,
particularly inflectional morphemes (Gumperz & Wilson, 1971;
Haugen, 1974). This finding is consistent with the idea that
each language is a structural system, characterized by redundancies between rules and consistencies across different rules
within the language. The tendency toward fusion threatens the
integrity of each language's overall structure.

The neutralization strategy which has been discussed in
the preceding section is a matter of simplification of the
structure *within* a language. Convergence and fusion are matters of simplification of structural rules *between* two or more
languages. These are presumed to be different processes, but
in the earliest stages of interlingual convergence the process
cannot be distinguished from neutralization. The earliest convergence changes do not necessarily threaten the integrity of
each language system, because they occur at the points of flexibility within each system. According to Weinreich (1953) the
reason modern Hebrew favors one of the two possible possessive
forms present in ancient Hebrew is that this particular form
is similar to the way the possessive is formed in Yiddish,
which many modern speakers of Hebrew also speak. In this case
convergence is merely a matter of favoring one of two existing
structural alternatives.

Ervin (1961b) offered evidence that semantic meanings may
fuse between languages. She found that bilinguals tend to
shift the semantic value of color words to lessen or remove
disagreement between the two languages. Macnamara (1967a) viewed this as reminiscent of Festinger's theory of cognitive dissonance, and to him it suggested that there is a strong pull

toward semantic fusion.

The less grasp a child has of the structures of both of his languages, the more easily should semantic merging occur for various types of words, content as well as function words. "Compound" bilinguals, as defined by Ervin and Osgood (1954) were bilinguals for whom the semantic meanings of words in their two languages were almost completely merged. The difference between these and "coordinate" bilinguals, for whom the meanings of words in the two languages are supposedly distinct, was attributed to whether or not the languages were learned in overlapping domains.

It is probably not accidental that the "compound" bilinguals they studied, who exhibited semantic merging, also tended, on the whole, to be rather poorly bilingual. The relative lack of mastery of the two languages' structures was probably responsible for the extensive semantic merging.

On the other hand, it is probably impossible not to have some semantic merging, especially with items high in referential content, even for bilinguals whose grasp of the two language structures is quite strong.

There are also some ways in which syntactic interaction between languages may occur in speech, as shown, for instance, in Haugen's review (1974). The most striking instance of syntactic merging which has been reported occurs at a communal level, in a situation in which multilingualism is a long-standing aspect of the society and in which most individuals are multilingual. Gumperz and Wilson (1971) claim that in the stable community they have examined, which has been multilingual for hundreds of years, the languages have converged in their very structure, even while lexical items have been kept quite distinct for intentional social reasons. If and when this does indeed occur, then the various cognitive advantages of bilingualism which have been hypothesized here as resulting from resistance to interlingual interference would no longer exist. It requires a linguist rather than a psychologist to properly evaluate Gumperz and Wilson's examples, but it can be noted that even though in these examples the word order of both languages does appear to have converged, inflectional morphemes are still quite different between languages.

It should be noted that in Gumperz and Wilson's example the syntactic merging — to whatever extent it has occurred — has come about as the result of social pressure existing over a long period of time and within a community in India where group relations are relatively static. According to these authors the social motivation for maintaining the languages as nominally separate from each other is to reinforce the social separation between the existing stable community groups. In this situation there seems to be little motivation for members of these groups to identify themselves with members of the oth-

er groups or to interact with each other except for limited
business purposes, much as in the standard pidgin-creole situation. One can infer that since there is not a strong need for
interaction between the language-culture groups except for limited purposes, there is also little need for strong maintenance
of the really basic structural distinctions between the languages. In this situation the psychological mechanisms which
help prevent interlingual interference do not need to operate.
The principle of least effort can prevail and the language can
be allowed to converge in structure, at least up to some point
at which the languages can still be identified as separate,
which the social situation demands. To the extent that syntactic merging does happen, the benefits which accrue to the
individual as a result of processes which arise to resist interlingual interference disappear. The benefits which occur
in this case are social benefits, since it is social pressure
that has brought about the merging.

　　In more usual situations of group contact the interaction
between groups is less set, and the sense of identity of the
persons involved in the interlingual-intercultural contact is
more at risk. In the United States, for example, there are
strong incentives to identify with the dominant culture group
as a means toward economic and social success, which brings the
individual up against the rejection by the dominant culture of
his native group and of the language which represents it. The
typical result has been predominance of the dominant culture
language in the immigrant's speech at the expense of deterioration and eventual loss of his native language. In this situation the two languages involved are not likely to converge much
because the rejecting attitudes of the dominant culture toward
signs of modification of its language by the immigrant group
or individual would counteract this tendency. In the process
of disintegration and abandonment, however, the native language
might increasingly manifest interference from the dominant culture language as well as general dedifferentiation as seen in
relative absence or instability of structural marking.

　　During this process the psychological mechanisms that
counteract interference, which have been described at length
in this chapter, function only to the extent that the native
language as well as the dominant culture language are both
still important to the individual for major aspects of his identity. Where the immigrant group with a different language happens to have high status in the dominant culture upon entry into it — a rare situation — or where the immigrant group can create for itself a protected environment in which children grow
up to respect both sets of values equally — a situation probably still not common, in spite of much recent support for the
value of ethnic identity in the United States — then the psychological mechanisms which maintain both languages as separate

structures by counteracting interlingual interference will
operate maximally.

REFERENCES

Anisfeld, M.E. A comparison of the cognitive functioning of
    monolinguals and bilinguals (Doctoral dissertation,
    McGill University, 1964).
Bellugi, U. Linguistic mechanisms underlying child speech.
    In E. Zale (Ed.), *Proceedings of the Conference on
    Language and Language Behavior*. Center for Research
    and Language Behavior. New York: Appleton-Century-
    Crofts, 1968.
Ben-Zeev, S. The influence of bilingualism on cognitive
    development and cognitive strategy (Doctoral disserta-
    tion, University of Chicago, 1972 ; available through
    University of Chicago photoduplication department).
Ben-Zeev, S. The effect of Spanish-English bilingualism in
    children from less privileged neighborhoods on cogni-
    tive development and cognitive strategy. Unpublished
    research report to National Institute of Child Health
    and Human Development, 1975.
Berko, J. The child's learning of English morphology.
    Word, 1958, *14,* 150-177.
Bruner, J., & Kenney, H. On multiple ordering. In J. Bruner,
    R. Olver, & P. Greenfield (Eds.), *Studies in cognitive
    growth*. New York: Wiley, 1966.
Burling, R. Language development of a Garo and English
    speaking child. *Word,* 1959, *15,* 45-68.
Clifton, C. The implications of grammar for word associa-
    tions. In K. Salzinger & S. Salzinger (Eds.), *Research
    in verbal behavior and some neurophysiological impli-
    cations*. New York: Academic Press, 1967.
Dale, P. *Language development: Structure and function*
    (2nd ed.). New York: Holt, Rinehart & Winston, 1976.
Darcy, N.T. A review of the literature on the effects of
    bilingualism upon the measurement of intelligence.
    Journal of Genetic Psychology, 1953, *82,* 21-57.
Ervin, S. Changes with age in the verbal determinants
    of word-associations. *American Journal of Psychology,*
    1961, *74,* 361-372. (a)
Ervin, S. Semantic shift in bilingualism. *American Journal
    of Psychology,* 1961, *74,* 233-241. (b)
Ervin, S. Correlates of associative frequency. *Journal of
    Verbal Learning and Verbal Behavior,* 1963, *1,* 422-431.

Ervin, S., & Osgood, C.E.   Second language learning and bilingualism. *Journal of Abnormal and Social Psychology* (Suppl.), 1954, *49*, 139-146.

Ervin-Tripp, S.   An overview of theories of grammatical development. In D. Slobin (Ed.), *The ontogenesis of grammar: A theoretical symposium*. New York: Academic Press, 1971.

Ervin-Tripp, S.   Some strategies for the first two years. In T. Moore (Ed.), *Cognitive development and the acquisition of language*. New York: Academic Press, 1973.

Genesee, F., Tucker, G.R., & Lambert, W.E.   Communication skills of bilingual children. *Child Development,* 1975, *46*, 1010-1014.

Greenberg, J.H.   *Essays in linguistics*. Chicago: University of Chicago Press, 1957.

Greenberg, J.H.   Some universals of grammar with particular reference to the order of meaningful elements. In J.H. Greenberg (Ed.), *Universals of language*. Cambridge, Mass.: M.I.T. Press, 1963.

Greenfield, P.   Goal as environmental variable in the development of intelligence. In R. Cancro (Ed.), *Intelligence: Genetic and environmental influences*. New York: Grune & Stratton, 1971.

Gumperz, J.J., & Wilson, R.   Convergence and creolization: A case from the Indo-Aryan/Dravidian border. In D. Hymes (Ed.), *Pidginization and creolization of languages*. Cambridge University Press, 1971.

Haugen, E.   Bilingualism, language contact, and immigrant languages in the U.S. In T. Sebeok (Ed.), *Current trends in linguistics* (Vol. 10). The Hague: Mouton, 1974.

Ianco-Worrall, A.   Bilingualism and cognitive development. *Child Development,* 1972, *43*, 1390-1400.

Inhelder, B. & Piaget, J.   *The early growth of logic in the child*. New York: Harper & Row, 1964.

Jenkins, J.J., & Palermo, D.S.   Mediation processes and the acquisition of linguistic structure. *Monographs of the Society for Research in Child Development,* 1964, *29* (1, 141-169).

Klima, E.S., & Bellugi, U.   Syntactic regularities in the speech of children. In J.L. Lyons & R.J. Wales (Eds.), *Psycholinguistic papers*. Edinburgh: Edinburgh University, Aldine Press, 1966.

Kolers, P.A.   Interlingual facilitation in short-term memory. *Journal of Verbal Learning and Verbal Behavior,* 1966, *5*, 314-139.

Lambert, W.E., Ignatow, M., & Krauthammer, M.   Bilingual organization in free recall. McGill University, 1966 (mimeo).

Lenneberg, E.H.   Language in the context of growth and matura-
     tion. *Biological foundations of language*. New York:
     Wiley, 1967. Chap. 4.
Macnamara, J.   The bilingual's linguistic performance — a psy-
     chological overview. In J. Macnamara (Ed.), Problems of
     bilingualism. *Journal of Social Issues,* 1967, *23,* (2),
     58-77. (a)
Macnamara, J.   The linguistic independence of bilinguals.
     Journal of Verbal Learning and Verbal Behavior, 1967,
     6, (5), 729-736. (b)
McNeill, D.   Developmental psycholinguistics. In F. Smith &
     G. Miller (Eds.), *The genesis of language*. Cambridge,
     Mass.: M.I.T. Press, 1966.
McNeill, D.   Development of the semantic system. Unpublished
     manuscript, 1971.
Moskowitz, A.I.   The two-year-old stage in the acquisition
     of English phonology. *Language,* 1970, *46,* 426-441.
Peal, E., & Lambert, W.   The relation of bilingualism to
     intelligence. *Psychological Monographs,* 1962, *76,*
     (27, Whole No. 546).
Penfield, W., & Roberts, L.   *Speech and brain mechanisms*.
     Princeton, N.J.: Princeton University Press, 1959.
Pfaff, C.   Constraints on code-switching. Paper presented
     at the meeting of the Chicago Linguistic Society,
     University of Chicago, April 1976.
Politzer, R.L., & Ramirez, A.G.   An error analysis of the
     spoken English of Mexican-American pupils in a bilin-
     gual school and a monolingual school. *Language Learn-
     ing,* 1973, *23,* No. 1, 43-61.
Preston, N.S.   *Interlingual interference in a bilingual
     version of the Stroop color-word test*. Unpublished
     Ph.D. thesis, McGill University, 1965.
Ravem, R.   Language acquisition in a second language en-
     vironment. *International Review of Applied Linguistics,*
     1968, *6,* 175-185.
Ronjat, J.   *Le développement du language observe chez un
     enfant bilingue*. Paris: Librarie Ancienne H. Champion,
     1913.
Selinker, L., Swain, M., & Dumas, G.   Interlanguage hypo-
     thesis extended to children. *Language Learning,* 1975,
     25, 139-152.
Stern, W.   *Die Erlernung und Beherrschung fremder Sprachen
     Zeitschrift fuer padagogesche Psychologie,* 1919, *20,*
     104-108.
Swain, M.   *Bilingual first-language acquisition: Comments
     made on the occasion of the International Symposium
     on First-Language Acquisition*, Florence, Italy,
     September, 1972. (a)

Swain, M. *Bilingualism as a first language.* Unpublished doctoral dissertation, University of California at Irvine, 1972. (b)

Torrance, E.P., Wu, J., Gowan, J.C., & Aliotti, N.C. Creative functioning of monolingual and bilingual children in Singapore. *Journal of Educational Psychology,* 1970, *61,* 72-75.

Warren, R.M., & Warren, R.P. A comparison of speech perception in childhood, maturity, and old age by means of the verbal transformation effect. *Journal of Verbal Learning and Verbal Behavior,* 1966, *5,* 142-146.

Weinreich, U. *Languages in contact.* New York: Linguistic Circle of New York, 1953.

Worrall, A. Bilingualism and cognitive development (Ph.D. dissertation, Cornell University, 1970; University Microfilm number DAI 31/04-B, order number 70-17472; published in part as article by A. Ianco-Worrall, cited above.)

Chapter 4

Bilingual Linguistic Memory:
The Independence-Interdependence
Issue Revisited

P.D. McCORMACK

Carleton University

Some investigators (e.g., Kolers, 1963; Tulving & Colotla, 1970) have suggested that bilingual memory may be represented by two functionally independent storage and retrieval systems, one for each language, that interact only through translation processes. These researchers, therefore, assume a two-store, or *independence,* position. Others (e.g., López and Young, 1974; Rose, et al., 1975), who are advocates of *interdependence,* state that all information exists in a single memory store. The purpose of this chapter is to examine those investigations most recently reported, as well as one which was overlooked in a previous literature review (McCormack, 1974), with the purpose of attempting to resolve the independence-interdependence issue. Five of these studies will be treated in detail and all will be seen to support the single-store model. Earlier studies, whose findings were previously interpreted as being more consistent with the two-store notion, will then be reexamined. It will be seen that these are also interpretable from an interdependence point of view, provided that it is assumed that memory for an event may be characterized by a complex of attributes or features (Anisfeld & Knapp, 1968; Bower, 1967; Hintzman, Block, & Innskeep, 1972; Underwood, 1969; Wickens, 1970), and that language is a relevant attribute whenever the to-be-remembered material is linguistically mixed.

The first study, the one that was overlooked in the earlier review, was reported by Young (1972), where a same-order serial transfer paradigm was employed. His subjects were exposed to a set of items in a constant serial order over a succession of trials. In this setting, the subjects must attempt to anticipate each item just prior to its presentation. They then learned a second list in which either synonyms, antonyms, or gender-related words were substituted for the first-list items; for example, "baby" in List 2 might replace "infant" in List 1, or "up" replace "down," or "brother" replace "sister." According to all extant theories of serial learning, positive transfer would be expected; that is, the subjects should learn the second list in fewer trials than a control group. For some, as yet unknown, reason no positive transfer was revealed. However, when the second-list items were translations of those from the first list, subjects fluent in both English and Spanish exhibited significant amounts of positive transfer (see Young & Saegert, 1966). These findings offer unambiguous support for the interdependence position.

The next investigation is one by López and Young (1974) who employed a multitrial free-recall procedure with English-Spanish bilinguals as subjects. In this setting, the subject is given a list of words and then must attempt to recall as many of them as possible. Unlike the serial-learning situation, the items appear in a different random sequence from trial to trial and the subject is free to recall them in any order. The procedure was one where the subjects had been familiarized with a particular set of words before being given the free-recall task. For the experimental conditions, the free-recall items were words which were translations of those with which the subject had been prefamiliarized. For the control treatments, the prefamiliarization set consisted of words from the same class as those employed for free recall, but a translation relationship did not exist. López and Young reasoned that, if the two linguistic systems are independent, then there should be no positive transfer from the first to the second task; that is, there should be no familiarization effect. However, positive transfer was demonstrated, and this was the case regardless of the language of the second task. The single-store notion, therefore, is supported once more.

The third investigation was conducted by Liepmann and Saegert (1974) whose subjects were familiar with both the Arabic and the English languages. The paradigm was that of Anderson and Bower (1972) where subjects are exposed only once to each list in a series, the requirement being that of free recall. With this paradigm, there is considerable overlap of the same words from list to list. Anderson and Bower report that recall becomes poorer as subjects are exposed to more and more lists and they attribute this to increasing amounts of confusion regarding list membership. The Liepmann-Saegert adaptation of the paradigm employed lists homogeneous and heterogeneous with respect to language. They reasoned that, if the interdependence notion is valid, performance should show a greater relative deterioration across trials when the lists are bilingual than when they are unilingual, since there should be two sources of confusion, one for language and one for list markers. On the other hand, should the independence notion make sense, subjects should show less relative deterioration on the bilingual lists, since they would be aided by being able to discriminate on the basis of language. In other words, the size of the word pool is effectively reduced by a factor of two. Their data were more consistent with the single memory-store position. Further support for this notion was revealed by the finding that more translation errors were observed as additional bilingual lists were encountered.

The fourth study was by Saegert, Kazarian, and Young (1973a) who employed a bilingually modified version of the part-whole negative transfer paradigm. In the part-whole setting, the subjects are first required to learn a "part" list and then a "whole" list which consists of the part-list items and an equal number of new items. In both tasks, the multi-trial free-recall procedure is employed. Negative transfer, namely poorer performance on the part of experimental subjects relative to appropriate controls, is typically observed on the second task. The reasons for this are probably the fractiona-tion of organizational units acquired during the learning of the "part" list as well as the necessity of reorganizing these items with the new words on the "whole" list (see Tulving, 1966). The modification devised by Saegert et al. (1973a) may be illustrated by briefly describing their experimental treat-ments. The subjects were English-Spanish bilinguals in one study and Arabic-English bilinguals in the other. They were given six trials of free recall from a unilingual "part" list, and then eleven trials from a "whole" list in the other lan-guage, half of the items being translations of those from the "part" list and half being new. In both experiments, negative part-whole transfer was observed only when the second list was composed of items from the weaker of the two languages. These findings are clearly consistent with the interdependence posi-tion, provided that Tulving's (1966) interpretation is valid. Negative transfer was not observed, however, when the second-list items were from the dominant language. This finding is clearly more consistent with the independence position which would predict no cross-language organization. Saegert et al. (1973a), however, did not appear to be overly concerned with this outcome, since they stated, although in a post hoc fash-ion, that weaker-language organizational units would be ex-pected to be difficult to form during the learning of the "part" list as well as easy to modify during the learning of the "whole" list, and so the outcome should be one of zero transfer.

The last of the recent investigations is one by Colletta (1975) in which a modification of Posner's (1969) "same-differ-ent" paradigm was employed. In this setting, the subject is

presented with two items and must judge whether they are the
same or different with respect to some predefined dimension.
The dependent variable in studies such as this is reaction
time, since performance is essentially errorless. Colletta's
subjects were English-French bilinguals and the dimension was
one of synonymity. For both "same" and "different" judgments,
the pairs of items were either homogeneous or heterogeneous
with respect to language. An example of a unilingual "same"
judgment might be BLACK-DARK, whereas a comparable bilingual
judgment might be either BLACK-NOIR or BLACK-FONCE. Similarly,
a unilingual "different" comparison might be BLACK-LAW with
the bilingual counterparts being BLACK-LOI and NOIR-LAW. Colletta reasoned that, should there be separate linguistic stores,
the bilingual judgments should produce longer reaction times
than the unilingual decisions, since a translation process
would presumably be required. Should there be a single memory
store, however, no differences in reaction time would be expected between the unilingual and bilingual conditions. The
latter was the case, in a setting likely characterized by adequate statistical power, and therefore his findings offer
strong, unambiguous support for the interdependence hypothesis.

Two other studies (López, Hicks, & Young, 1974; Weist &
Crawford, 1972) were reported subsequent to the earlier review
(McCormack, 1974). Both support the interdependence position
but they will not be treated at this time. Two additional investigations, the findings of which are not of direct rele-
vance to the issue, were also reported during this period (Mc-
Cormack & Colletta, 1975; Yadrick & Kausler, 1974). They are
included in the reference list so that the reader will have,
with the two literature reviews available, an up-to-date bibliography of the bilingual-memory literature.

Those studies reviewed earlier, the findings of which were
interpreted as supporting the two-store position, will now be
briefly reevaluated. In the first of these, Kolers (1964) required his subjects to practice saying either their native alphabet or the English alphabet backwards, and then tested them
on the other. There was no evidence of positive transfer
across languages, which led him to opt for two independent linguistic systems that are probably "insulated from each other."
The reliability of these data, however, is questionable since
Dalrymple-Alford (1967) obtained positive transfer in a somewhat similar setting. The second study is one by Tulving and
Colotla (1970) who had their subjects recall freely from unilingual, bilingual, or trilingual lists, their languages being
English, French, and Spanish. Recall was best from unilingual
lists, next best from bilingual lists, and poorest from trilingual lists. These investigators interpreted the poorer recall from multilingual lists as reflecting an impairment in the
organization of words across language boundaries. Their data

are, therefore, consistent with the notion that the two languages of a bilingual person, or the three of a trilingual,
normally "exist in relative isolation" from one another. Although these data support the independence position, they appear to be atypical, since all of the remaining free-recall
studies have failed to detect any performance differences between unilingual and bilingual conditions (Kolers, 1965; Lambert, Ignatow, & Krauthamer, 1968; Liepmann & Saegert, 1974;
Nott & Lambert, 1968; Saegert, Obermeyer, & Kazarian, 1973).
McCormack and Novell (1975) have also recently failed to find
any differences in recall from secondary (long-term) memory between unilingual and trilingual treatments. It is also worth
mentioning that the Tulving-Colotla subjects were required to
learn overlapping lists much like those employed by Liepmann
and Saegert (1974). It is, therefore, not surprising that performance deteriorated as a function of the degree to which the
lists were heterogeneous with respect to language. The third
investigation was one by Saegert, Obermeyer, and Kazarian
(1937b) who employed a bilingually modified version of the
whole-part negative transfer paradigm. The "whole" list consisted of an equal number of items from both the English and
the Arabic languages, whereas the "part" list was composed of
the English whole-list items for one group of subjects and the
Arabic whole-list items for another. Control subjects experienced "part" lists made up of items being encountered for the
first time. Negative transfer was obtained but only where the
"part" list was in Arabic. They interpreted these findings as
indicative of cross-language organization during the acquisition of the bilingual "whole" list and, therefore, as being
consistent with the interdependence, or single-store, position.
Their failure to find negative transfer in the English part-
list condition was cited in the earlier review (McCormack,
1974) as being more consistent with the two-store model. However, Saegert and his colleagues present a reasonably sound,
although again *post hoc,* argument for why their prediction
failed. Their overall interpretation of the data, therefore,
is one which utilizes the interdependence model.

The findings of the two remaining investigations, although
consistent with the two-store model, might instead be more par-
simoniously interpreted as establishing language as a relevant
attribute of memory in settings where the materials are linguistically mixed. There is no point in invoking two memory
stores when one will suffice. A similar argument, with respect to the short-term versus long-term memory controversy,
is attracting increasing attention (Cermak, 1972; Craik & Lockhart, 1972; Herriot, 1974; Melton, 1963; Murdock, 1974). In
the first of these two studies, Goggin and Wickens (1971) employed English-Spanish bilingual subjects who were given three
consecutive tests for short-term retention of strings of four-
letter words in either English or Spanish. Performance deteri-

orated across tests, reflecting the accumulation of the effects
of proactive interference (PI). On the fourth test, the experimental groups were shifted to items from the other language
while the control subjects continued on with words in the same
language. These investigators reasoned that, if different languages have separate memory stores, then a change in language
should produce almost complete "release from PI." If, on the
other hand, the languages share a common memory store, then
the amount of "release" should be negligible. Substantial
amounts of "release from PI" were observed and so the data are
clearly consistent with the independence position. Similar
findings have been reported by Dillon *et al*. (1973). The results of these two studies, may, however, be more sensibly interpreted as demonstrating language as a memorial attribute.
In fact, this is the commonly accepted interpretation of the
release phenomenon whenever it is observed in linguistically
homogeneous settings (see Wickens, 1970). The phenomenon is
used as evidence that the category presented during the accumulation of interference and the category used on the "release"
trial are perceived as being psychologically dissimilar. In
other words, the two categories are differentially encodable
and, hence, an attribute of memory has been identified. The
last study, one by Glanzer and Duarte (1971), was concerned
with items that are presented twice in a single-trial free-recall setting. The manipulation of interest, in studies such
as this one, is lag; that is, the number of items which inter-
vene between the first and second presentation of an item.
The typical finding is that recall is an increasing function
of lag, and one interpretation of these data is that, with increased separation of repetition, there is a corresponding increase in the probability of two contextual codings of an item
(see Martin, 1968; Melton, 1967). Two encodings presumably
provide two retrieval routes to a long-lag item and thus facilitate its recall. It, therefore, follows that recall should
be invariant with lag whenever two encodings are achieved for
all words. Under such circumstances, massed as well as spaced
items should be accessible by either of two retrieval routes
(see McCormack & Carboni, 1973). Glanzer and Duarte employed
a bilingual modification of the paradigm, whereby an item was
presented in English on one occasion and in Spanish on another.
Although probability of recall was not invariant with lag, the
effect was considerably attenuated. These data, therefore,
appear to support a position halfway between that of independence and interdependence. A more sensible interpretation would
simply be one which accounts for the superior performance in
the mixed-language condition in terms of the opportunity to
utilize the linguistic attribute. Paivio (1975), however, has
recently reported data from an unpublished experiment which are
more in line with the two-store model. In this study, subjects

transcribed an equal number of English and French words into English and then were given an unexpected test of free recall of all words. The proportion of translated words recalled was .34, whereas that for the copied set was only .17. These data are clearly consistent with the notion that two linguistic stores were independently accessed in the translated-word condition and should be given careful attention when they appear in published form.

One of the more convincing sources of support for the notion of language as an encoding attribute is the consistent finding that subjects are able to identify the input language of an item at the point of its recall from a mixed-language list (Kolers, 1965; Lambert, Ignatow, & Krauthamer, 1968; Nott and Lambert, 1968). Their ability to do so is at a level far exceeding that which would be expected by chance. Three recent studies have confirmed these findings and have extended them to the recognition-memory setting as well (Rose & Carroll, 1974; Rose, Rose, King, & Perez, 1975; Saegert, Hamayan, & Ahmar, 1975). Two of these will be examined briefly. In the first, Rose, *et al.* (1975) presented their subjects with sentences, some in English and some in Spanish, and then later tested them for either recognition or recall. When the sentence was correctly recalled it was typically output in the language of input. Also the subjects had little difficulty in recognizing the fact that the sentence had been presented in one language and not in the other. These investigators interpret their findings as being consistent with the notion that memory traces are formed from ensembles of features or attributes. Rose *et al.* are, therefore, able to retain the single-store model, yet, at the same time, account for the ease with which subjects can tag by language. In the other study, Saegert, Hamayan, and Ahmar (1975) employed Arabic-English-French trilinguals as subjects. Either single words or sentences appeared at input, the languages being English and French. A recognition test followed in which single items were presented in Arabic. These words were either "targets" or "distractors"; that is, they had or had not been shown previously. Consistent with the findings of other investigators was the observation that, given correct recognition, the input language could be readily identified. Also, language tagging was better for words presented alone at input than for items which had been embedded in sentences. Saegert, *et al.* also favor a single-store model with language as an encoding attribute. According to these investigators, subjects selectively attend to the attributes and, when single words are presented, the subject will be more likely to attend to language than he would when the words are embedded in sentences. In the latter situation, the semantic attributes would, presumably, dominate the nonsemantic ones.

Only thirteen years have elapsed since Kolers (1963) raised the independence-interdependence issue. During that brief
period of time, sufficient data have been collected to enable
us to conclude that the single-store position makes most sense,
both in terms of parsimony and in terms of its predictive and
explanatory power. The game, which we call science, rarely re-
veals such rapid progress. Ebbinghaus (1885) began it all less
than a century ago, and, in our more pessimistic moments, we
are sometimes heard to say that our body of knowledge has not
expanded perceptibly in that period. You will infer correctly
that I am feeling somewhat optimistic when I say that we will
eventually define the problems, as well as state the benefits,
of bilingualism as it affects the individual and the society.

REFERENCES

Anderson, J.R., & Bower, G.H. Recognition and retrieval pro-
    cesses in free recall. *Psychological Review,* 1972, *79,*
    97-123.
Anisfeld, M., & Knapp, M.E. Association, synonymity and
    directionality in false recognition. *Journal of Experi-
    mental Psychology,* 1968, *77,* 171-179.
Bower, G.H. A multicomponent theory of the memory trace.
    In K.W. Spence & J.T. Spence (Eds.), *The psychology
    of learning and motivation* (Vol. 1). New York:
    Academic Press, 1967.
Cermak, L.S. *Human memory: Research and theory.* New York:
    Ronald Press, 1972.
Colletta, S.P. "Same-different" judgments with bilinguals.
    Unpublished M.A. thesis, Carleton University, 1975.
Craik, F.I.M., & Lockhart, R.S. Levels of processing:
    A framework for memory research. *Journal of Verbal
    Learning and Verbal Behavior,* 1972, *11,* 671-684.
Dalrymple-Alford, E. Interlingual transfer of training.
    Psychonomic Science, 1967, *8,* 167-168.
Dillon, R.F., McCormack, P.D., Petrusic, W.M., Cook, G.M.,
    & Lafleur, L. Release from proactive interference in
    compound and coordinate bilinguals. *The Bulletin of
    the Psychonomic Society, 1973, 2,* 293-294.
Ebbinghaus, H. *Memory: A contribution to experimental
    psychology.* (H.A. Ruger & C.E. Bussenius, trans.).
    New York: Dover, 1964.
Glanzer, M., & Duarte, A. Repetition between and within
    languages in free recall. *Journal of Verbal Learning
    and Verbal Behavior,* 1971, *10,* 625-630.

Goggin, J., & Wickens, D.D. Proactive interference and language change in short-term memory. *Journal of Verbal Learning and Verbal Behavior*, 1971, *10*, 453-458.

Herriot, P. *Attributes of memory*. London: Methuen, 1974.

Hintzman, D.L., Block, R.A., & Innskeep, N.R. Memory for mode of input. *Journal of Verbal Learning and Verbal Behavior*, 1972, *11*, 741-749.

Kolers, P.A. Interlingual word association. *Journal of Verbal Learning and Verbal Behavior*, 1963, *2*, 291-300.

Kolers, P.A. Specificity of a cognitive operation. *Journal of Verbal Learning and Verbal Behavior*, 1964, *3*, 244-248.

Kolers, P.A. Bilingualism and biocodalism. *Language and Speech*, 1965, *8*, 122-126.

Lambert, W.E., Ignatow, M., & Krauthamer, M. Bilingual organization in free recall. *Journal of Verbal Learning and Verbal Behavior*, 1968, *7*, 207-214.

Liepmann, D., & Saegert, J. Language tagging in bilingual free recall. *Journal of Experimental Psychology*, 1974, *103*, 1137-1141.

López, M., Hicks, R.E., & Young, R.K. Retroactive inhibition in a bilingual A-B, A-B' paradigm. *Journal of Experimental Psychology*, 1974, *103*, 85-90.

López, M., & Young, R.K. The linguistic interdependence of bilinguals. *Journal of Experimental Psychology*, 1974, *102*, 981-983.

Martin, E. Stimulus meaningfulness and paired-associate transfer: An encoding variability hypothesis. *Psychological Review*, 1968, *75*, 421-441.

McCormack, P.D. Bilingual linguistic memory: Independence or interdependence; two stores or one? In S.T. Carey (Ed.), *Bilingualism, biculturalism and education*. Edmonton: University of Alberta Printing Department, 1974.

McCormack, P.D., & Carboni, N.L. Lag invariance with forced encodings in free recall. *Canadian Journal of Psychology*, 1973, *27*, 144-151.

McCormack, P.D., & Colletta, S.P. Recognition memory for items from unilingual and bilingual lists. *The Bulletin of the Psychonomic Society*, 1975, *6*, 149-151.

McCormack, P.D., & Novell, J.A. Free recall from unilingual and trilingual lists. *The Bulletin of the Psychonomic Society*, 1975, *6*, 173-174.

Melton, A.W. Implications of short-term memory for a general theory of memory. *Journal of Verbal Learning and Verbal Behavior*, 1963, *2*, 1-21.

Melton, A.W. Repetition and retrieval from memory. *Science*, 1967, *158*, 532.

Murdock, B.B., Jr.   *Human memory: Theory and data.* New York: Wiley, 1974.

Nott, C.R., & Lambert, W.E.   Free recall of bilinguals. *Journal of Verbal Learning and Verbal Behavior,* 1968, *7,* 1065-1071.

Paivio, A.   Coding distinctions and repetition effects in memory. In G.H. Bower (Ed.), *The psychology of learning and motivation* (Vol. 9). New York: Academic Press, 1975.

Posner, M.I.   Abstraction and the process of recognition. In G.H. Bower & J.T. Spence (Eds.), *The psychology of learning and motivation* (Vol. 3). New York: Academic Press, 1969.

Rose, R.G., & Carroll, J.F.   Free recall of a mixed-language list. *Bulletin of the Psychonomic Society,* 1974, *3,* 267-268.

Rose, R.G., Rose, P.R., King, N., & Perez, A.   Bilingual memory for related and unrelated sentences. *Journal of Experimental Psychology: Human Learning and Memory,* 1975, *1,* 599-606.

Saegert, J., Hamayan, E., & Ahmar, H.   Memory for language of input in polygots. *Journal of Experimental Psychology: Human Learning and Memory,* 1975, *1,* 607-613.

Saegert, J., Kazarian, S., & Young, R.K.   Part/whole transfer with bilinguals. *American Journal of Psychology,* 1973a, *86,* 537-546.

Saegert, J., Obermeyer, J., & Kazarian, S.   Organizational factors in free recall of bilingually-mixed lists. *Journal of Experimental Psychology,* 1973b, *97,* 397-399.

Tulving, E.   Subjective organization and effects of repetition in multi-trial free-recall learning. *Journal of Verbal Learning and Verbal Behavior,* 1966, *5,* 193-197.

Tulving, E., & Colotla, V.A.   Free recall of bilingual lists. *Cognitive Psychology,* 1970, *1,* 86-98.

Underwood, B.J.   Attributes of memory. *Psychological Review,* 1969, *76,* 559-573.

Weist, R.M., & Crawford, C.   Phonological and semantic representations of words, compartments of memory and rehearsal. *Psychonomic Science,* 1972, *28,* 106-108.

Wickens, D.D.   Encoding categories of words: An empirical approach to meaning. *Psychological Review,* 1970, *77,* 1-15.

Yadrick, A.M., & Kausler, D.H.   Verbal discrimination learning for bilingual lists. *Journal of Experimental Psychology,* 1974, *102,* 899-900.

Young, R.K.   Transfer in serial learning. In C.P. Duncan, L. Sechrest, & A.W. Melton (Eds.), *Human memory.* New York: Appleton-Century-Crofts, 1972.

Young, R.K., & Saegert, J.   Transfer with bilinguals. *Psychonomic Science,* 1966, *6,* 161-162.

Chapter 5

Bilingualism and
Intergroup Relations

DONALD M. TAYLOR

McGill University

The question I would like to address is, how can effective
interaction in a multilingual environment be facilitated? Two
requirements seem necessary to achieve such a goal. First,
people must have the ability to interact. That is, they must
attain a degree of bilingualism that will at least permit interaction. Second, people must be motivated to interact. Giv-
en the prerequisite of the first, it is clear that a motivation for interaction will involve some desire to attain a degree of fluency in the second language. Despite the anxiety
expressed over the limitations of second-language teaching, I
believe that in most cases this is not the major barrier to interaction. Students who emerge from second-language training
programs appear more capable than either they or their teachers appreciate. Support for this contention comes from a series of experiments with which I have been involved in Manitoba,
in Quebec, and in the Philippines (see Taylor & Simard, 1975
for review). In these experiments members of two ethnolinguistic groups were required to perform a series of tasks requiring effective communication. Although all participants had received only the normal second-language instruction prescribed
in primary and secondary school, they were capable of communicating effectively with each other.

Furthermore, significant advances in methods of second-
language instruction, and here I refer specifically to the very
innovative social experiments of Lambert and Tucker and their
colleagues (see Lambert & Tucker, 1972), lead me to feel confident that second-language abilities can be taught effectively.

The key to promoting effective interethnic group interaction hinges then upon the motivations of the members of both

groups. The issue centers on the dynamics of intergroup relations, and it is the motivational consequences of these relations as they involve language that are the focus of this chapter. Specifically, I want to discuss three motivational issues
related to bilingualism and intergroup relations: (1) how, for
less powerful groups, bilingualism may affect a person's relationship with his own group — ethnic identity; (2) how, for
more powerful groups, attitudes toward second-language learning may be changed; and (3) how the bilingual's choice of language can be used to express cooperation or hostility in intergroup relations.

ETHNIC IDENTITY

Learning a second language involves far more than the acquisition of a new set of symbols for communication. Aside
from a host of potential cognitive and intellectual consequences there are important social consequences as well. Where two
or more ethnolinguistic groups exist in an unequal relationship,
second-language learning will have important implications for
ethnic identity, particularly for the less powerful group.
The importance of this relationship has perhaps, until recently, not been fully appreciated. We have conducted a number of
studies which represent initial attempts to examine this issue
(Taylor, Simard, & Aboud, 1972; Taylor, Bassili, & Aboud, 1973;
Giles, Taylor, & Bourhis, in press). French and English Que-
becers for example, maintain distinct and separate patterns of
identity and, for both groups, *language,* even more than cultural background, is the major feature of this identity. Thus,
French-Canadian respondents identify more with an English Canadian who speaks French mainly, than with a French Canadian
who speaks English mainly. This latter group, that is French
Canadians who speak mainly English, received extreme reactions
from our French-Canadian respondents. It was as if they were
judged to be traitors, members of the group who had "sold out"
to the English. This reaction points clearly to the important
relationship between second-language learning and ethnic identity. Further, in a study of Welsh identity, language again
emerged as the most salient feature of identity. This is not
to suggest that language is the only dimension of identity but
only to point out that a person's language repertoire will have
important implications for ethnic identity.
A recent study conducted by Frasure-Smith, Lambert, and
Taylor (1975) illustrates this point clearly. We wondered
whether French-speaking parents who send their children to an
English school would have a pattern of ethnic identity which
is different from those whose children attend the regular
French school. All the parents saw Quebec society as compris-

ed of three major groups — monolingual English Canadians, monolingual French Canadians, and a third group composed of both
bilingual French Canadians and bilingual English Canadians.
The parents whose children attended the French school identified strongly with the "monolingual French group" and felt
equally removed from both the monolingual English group and
the French and English bilingual groups. Further, this group
of parents identified strongly with their children who they
felt were identifying mainly with the monolingual French group.

By contrast, parents who had decided on English-language
schooling for their children showed a different pattern of
identity. These parents were not closely aligned with monolingual French Canadians and evidenced some identity with the
bilingual French and English groups. In addition these parents identified less with their children who they perceived to
be even closer to the bilingual groups than themselves. It
would seem that learning a second language, in this case by
having one's children attend the "other" language school, has
important implications for ethnic identity. Parents who make
this choice have pulled away from an identity with a monolingual French group and seem to have shifted their identity toward bilingual French and English groups. Further, this choice
of schooling in English seems to have separated, to some extent, children from their parents in terms of ethnic identity.

This apparent shift in identity has serious social impli-
cations. French Canada has been described as a "seige culture"
(Baker, 1973), a term meant to characterize the struggle by
French Canadians for the preservation of ethnic identity in the
face of Anglo and American domination and assimilation. If
French Canadians are anxious to maintain a solid French iden-
tity, then, as we have seen, having their children attend an
English-language school may seriously undermine this goal.

Threats to ethnic identity, which arise from inequalities
in intergroup relations may alter the motivational balance for
becoming bilingual. In order to examine this issue Taylor,
Meynard, and Rheault (in press) asked a sample of 246 French-
Canadian college students about their bilingual skills and
their feelings about learning English. Specifically we asked
respondents to rate:

1. How much contact they had with English Canadians.
2. To what extent learning English constituted a threat
   to various aspects of their ethnic identity (e.g.,
   likelihood of assimilation, increased anonymity).
3. The extent of their agreement with favorable instrumental rewards, such as financial benefits, better
   jobs, which accrue from learning English.
4. The extent of their agreement with favorable integrative reasons, such as interactions with the Eng-

lish, openness toward other cultures, for learning
English.

Although a number of studies have pointed to the importance of instrumental and integrative motivations for success
in second-language learning (Gardner & Lambert, 1972), this
study showed that the two variables related to intergroup relations, that is contact and threat to ethnic identity, were
the two most important factors in predicting level of second-
language ability. This does not suggest that instrumental and
integrative motivations are unimportant but only that motivations stemming from the consequences of intergroup relations
are also central to promoting bilingualism. Thus, in our
study, personal contact with English Canadians was associated
with fluency in English and feeling one's ethnic identity
threatened served as a deterrent to bilingualism.

Our study also explored how contact with members of a majority group affects ethnic identity. We hypothesized that
French Canadians who have contact with English Canadians, as
is the case in Montreal, would feel their identity more threatened than those who live outside Montreal and hence have little
or no contact with English-speaking persons. The results were
contrary to our prediction. Where contact was high, there was
little fear of identity loss in general, and certainly no special concern about the effect of learning English on one's ethnic identity. We can only speculate that, contrary to our initial hypothesis, contact with a group provides the experience
which is necessary to render them less threatening.

There is then an important relationship between second-
language learning and ethnic identity, especially for members
of less powerful ethnolinguistic groups. The success or failure of second-language programs is not limited to instructional and learner characteristics, account must also be taken of
the intergroup relations context within which a second-language program operates.

LANGUAGE ATTITUDES

For members of more powerful ethnolinguistic groups positive attitudes toward the other group are essential for promoting bilingualism. Most ethnolinguistic groups are ethno-
centric (Sumner, 1906), group members believing that characteristics of their culture, customs, and language are better
than others. In situations of intergroup competition or conflict, ethnocentrism is enhanced (see LeVine, 1965) with the
result that members of one group have negative attitudes about
members of the other group and the language they speak. Such
circumstances clearly provide a poor basis for promoting bilin-

gualism.

A study by Garg, Inder, Shekar, & Taylor (1972) demonstrates how intergroup competition affects attitudes toward language directly. The context of the study was south India where the attitudes of native Kannada speakers toward the languages of rival outgroups were studied. As a first step, ten Indian professors of linguistics rated several languages in terms of their similarity to Kannada. These linguists rated Telegu and Tamil to be highly similar to Kannada, and Hindi and English to be extremely different. We then asked a sample of native Kannada speakers from the city of Mysore to perform the same task. These people judged Telegu and Tamil, the languages of two of their rival outgroups, to be very different from Kannada, and Hindi and English to be similar. Kannada speakers then accentuated whatever differences existed between their language and those of rival outgroups and then used this to explain their inability to perform in these languages.

How then can attitudes be changed? Traditional social psychological theory advocates implicitly that attitudes are the cause of behavior. Hence in a situation of intergroup competition the attitudes of the more powerful group should be changed and this should lead to a greater motivation to learn the language of the other group. According to this view legislating a language policy with a view to promoting bilingualism will yield little or no effective results; in Sumner's (1906) words, "Stateways cannot change folkways." Attitudes should be changed first, and then legislation may follow which will reflect this change in attitude.

A number of social scientists (e.g., Aronson, 1972; Allport, 1954; Bem, 1970; Colombotos, 1969) have questioned seriously this traditional cause-effect relationship, and this alternative view has important implications for promoting bilingualism. A number of experiments demonstrate that if a person, for one reason or another, behaves in a manner which is inconsistent with his attitudes, then the person's attitudes will change to become consonant with the behavior. If a prejudiced English Canadian is forced through legislation to use French, then the person will be forced to resolve dissonance: I dislike the French language but I am learning it and will use it. In order to resolve this dissonance our English Canadian can either not speak French or change his prejudices. Since speaking French is enforced through legislation, the only alternative for our English Canadian is to change his attitudes about French Canadians and the prospects of speaking French.

At least two qualifications are necessary to this rather simple interpretation. In the first place our English Canadian may have rehearsed prior to the legislation his reaction to being forced to change his attitudes, and this form of "inoculation" (McGuire, 1964) may make him resistant to attitude

change. Second, an English Canadian's negative attitudes about
using French may not be inconsistent with the fact that he actually uses French since he may attribute the use of French to
external (legislation) rather than internal (self-motivated)
causes. The result may be a "backlash" such that negative attitudes become even more firmly entrenched.

These qualifications notwithstanding, it does seem that
behavior can influence attitudes. Thus, rather than intro-
ducing an education campaign designed to change language attitudes, it would seem more profitable to reverse the procedure
on the assumption that "one of the most effective ways to
'change the hearts and minds of men' is to change their behavior" (Bem, 1970, p. 54).

INTERPERSONAL ACCOMMODATION THROUGH LANGUAGE

Thus far, our discussion has focused on aspects of intergroup relations which affect the learning of a second language
by both powerful and less powerful social groups. We turn now
to how bilinguals from both groups may use their language capa-
bilities to express cooperation and conflict in intergroup relations. Giles (1973) has formulated a theory of accommodation
which suggests that if a person adjusts his speech style to be
more similar to that of another (convergence) the result will
be a favorable reaction by the "other" and reciprocated accommodation. Conversely, a person may modify his speech style in
a direction opposite to that of the other, and this divergence
would be interpreted negatively by the "other" and evoke a divergent speech style in return. Thus, language style may be
used as a mechanism for inducing cooperation or conflict.

In order to test the theory in a bilingual context, Giles,
Taylor, and Bourhis (1973) had a French Canadian prepare three
tape-recorded messages for English Canadians. In one message
the French-Canadian speaker accommodated to his English-Canadian listener by speaking English. The second message involved
partial accommodation in that the message contained a mixture
of French and English. For the third message the French Canadian did not accommodate and presented his message in French.
Our English-Canadian listeners were presented with one of the
three messages and were then asked to evaluate the speaker.
They were then given the opportunity to tape-record a message
of their own back to the speaker. We predicted first, that the
more the French-Canadian speaker accommodated to the English-
Canadian listener the more favorably the speaker would be eval-
uated and, second, that the more the French-Canadian speaker
accommodated, the more the English Canadian would accommodate
back to the speaker.

The results confirmed both hypotheses. The more the

French Canadian accommodated the more he was judged favorably especially in terms of his "considerateness" and his efforts "to bridge the cultural gap." When the French Canadian chose not to accommodate, by speaking French, the English Canadian tended to return the message in English. When the speaker used a mixture of French and English he received the same in return. Finally, when the French Canadian accommodated by speaking English, the English Canadian subjects attempted to reciprocate by speaking French. These findings demonstrate how a bilingual's choice of language may be used to foster cooperation or conflict in intergroup relations. The accommodation situation is especially interesting since both the French Canadian and the English Canadian were using their second language, choosing to express cooperation at the expense of communication efficiency. We have since had the opportunity to replicate and extend (Simard, Taylor, & Giles, in press) these findings, this time using English-Canadian speakers and French-Canadian listeners. This study supported the earlier findings in that accommodation was effective in terms of evoking the expected speaker evaluations and reciprocal accommodation.

Clearly in an intergroup situation members of both groups make important attributions of the intentions of others based on language choice. The bilingual is in an especially important position because of his or her capacity for inducing cooperation. Obviously a monolingual person does not have such a capacity, and indeed may have already communicated, by a lack of second-language fluency, a nonaccommodating message to members of the other group.

CONCLUSIONS

The major thrust of the present argument is that in some situations second-language learning and use must be understood within the context of intergroup relations. The motivational balance for learning a second language and making use of these skills once they have been acquired is a delicate one. For some, the positive instrumental and integrative rewards which accrue from becoming bilingual may be overshadowed by the threat second-language learning poses for ethnic identity. For others it may be that a major barrier to bilingualism is negative attitudes toward members of the other group. Finally, the acquisition of a second language and the bilinguals' choice of language can be used to promote cooperation or conflict in intergroup interaction.

REFERENCES

Allport, G.W. *The nature of prejudice.* Cambridge, Mass.:
    Addison Wesley, 1954.
Aronson, E. *The social animal.* San Francisco: W.H. Freeman,
    1972.
Baker, D.G. Ethnicity, development and power: Canada in
    comparative perspective. Paper presented at National
    Conference on Canadian Cultural and Ethnic Groups in
    Canada, Toronto, October, 1973.
Bem, D.J. *Beliefs, attitudes and human affairs.* Belmont,
    Calif.: Wadsworth, 1970.
Colombotos, J. Physicians and medicare: A before-after
    study of the effects of legislation on attitudes.
    American Sociological Review, 1969, *34,* 318-334.
Frasure-Smith, N.E., Lambert, W.E., & Taylor, D.M.
    Choosing the language of instruction for one's children:
    A Quebec study. *Journal of Cross-cultural Psychology,*
    1975, *6,* 131-155.
Gardner, R.C., & Lambert, W.E. *Attitudes and motivation in
    second-language learning.* Rowley, Mass.: Newbury House,
    1972.
Garg, R.C., Inder, S., Shekar, R., & Taylor, D.M. Perception
    of language similarities in a social context. Mimeo.
    Central Institute of Indian Languages, Mysore, 1972.
Giles, H. Accent mobility: model and some data. *Anthropo-
    logical Linguistics,* 1973, *15,* 87-105.
Giles, H.M., Taylor, D.M., & Bourhis, R. Towards a theory
    of interpersonal accommodation through language: a
    Canadian data. *Language in Society,* 1973, *2,* 177-192.
Giles, H.M., Taylor, D.M., & Bourhis, R. Dimensions of
    Welsh identity. *European Journal of Social Psychology,*
    in press.
Lambert, W.E., & Tucker, G.R. *Bilingual education of children:
    St. Lambert experiment.* Rowley, Mass.: Newbury House,
    1972.
LeVine, R.A. Socialization, social structure and inter-
    societal images. In H.C. Kelman (Ed.), *International
    behavior: a social-psychological analysis.* New York:
    Holt, Rinehart & Winston, 1965.
McGuire, J.W. Inducing resistance to persuasion: Some
    contemporary approaches. In L. Berkowitz (Ed.),
    Advances in experimental social psychology (Vol. 1).
    New York: Academic Press, 1964.
Simard, L.M., Taylor, D.M., & Giles, H. Attribution processes
    and interpersonal accommodation in a bilingual setting.
    Language and Speech, in press.

Sumner, W.G. *Folkways*. New York: The New American Library, 1906.

Taylor, D.M., Bassili, J.N., & Aboud, F.E.   Dimensions of ethnic identity: An example from Quebec. *Journal of Social Psychology*, 1973, *89*, 185-192.

Taylor, D.M., Meynard, R., & Rheault, E.   Threat to Ethnic Identity and Second-Language Learning. In H. Giles (Ed.), *Language, ethnicity and intergroup relations*. London: Academic Press, in press.

Taylor, D.M., & Simard, L.M.   Social interaction in a bilingual setting. *Canadian Psychological Review*, 1975, *16*, 240-254.

Taylor, D.M., Simard, L.M., & Aboud, F.E.   Ethnic identification in Canada: A cross-cultural investigation. *Canadian Journal of Behavioural Sciences*, 1972, *4*, 13-20.

Chapter 6

Studies of the Nonfluent Bilingual

NORMAN SEGALOWITZ   ELIZABETH GATBONTON

Concordia University   *McGill University*

We define the nonfluent bilingual as the second-language
user who possesses sufficient skill with a language for successful basic communication but who nevertheless is perceived
by others and by himself as not possessing nativelike control
of the language. Most studies of bilingual populations have
paid little attention to nonfluent speakers, but there are
several reasons why more work should be devoted to them.
First, in many if not most regions of the world where second-
language users are found, nonfluent speakers outnumber the fluent bilinguals. In this respect the nonfluent second-language
user may be a more typical, if not ideal, representative of bilinguals. In addition, insofar as bilingualism studies aim to
increase our understanding of second-language acquisition, they
ought to provide analyses that encompass speakers with a variety of levels of skill in the second language. In this chapter
we would like to describe some of our work that has focused on
the nonfluent bilingual.

    There are three main issues we have tried to explore with
respect to such bilinguals. The first is whether they share
a common speech code. Second-language-using populations include many speakers of different levels of proficiency, and
the speech pattern of a group as a whole may not be readily
viewed as comprising a single speech code because of its extreme heterogeneity. The second issue we have focused upon is
how nonfluent second-language users might be affected by sociolinguistic norms governing the use of particular speech styles
in particular situations. Finally, we have explored the issue
of whether members of bilingual populations share certain attitudes about the social implications of speaking in particular
ways.

    These three issues — shared speech code, sociolinguistic

77

rules for speech use, and shared attitudes about speech — have
been central to many studies of mother-tongue-speech communities (Gumperz, 1972; Hymes, 1971; Labov, 1970). In exploring
these topics with respect to populations of second-language
speakers we have made no attempt to answer the question of
whether such groups actually constitute true speech communities.
In some cases they very well may and in some they clearly do
not. Rather, we have chosen to focus upon these issues in our
studies mainly because their investigation has proven very
fruitful in the study of mother-tongue groups and it seemed
worthwhile, therefore, to explore them in relation to second-
language users.

THE POPULATIONS

    The groups of bilinguals that have been the focus of our
studies are Francophone and Anglophone second-language users
in Quebec. Three features of these groups need to be mention-
ed here so that the similarities and differences between these
groups and others that have been investigated may be better
appreciated.
    First, the majority of bilinguals in each group do not
speak the second language fluently. Most have abilities that
may be described as ranging from minimal to almost nativelike;
relatively few would be classified as nativelike in the second
language.
    Second, each second-language-using population itself is a
distinct subset of the mother-tongue group. For example, only
some Anglophones can manage to any extent in French and, by
and large, most Anglophones are not even functionally bilingual. Similarly, not all Francophones have functional skills
in English (although it is probably true that in Quebec propor-
tionately more Francophones than Anglophones are bilingual).
This point is important because it means that the second-language users within each group have linguistic skills which are
by no means universal to the group and thus, to an extent,
they are set apart from the rest of the mother-tongue community.
    Third, the speakers in our studies use their second lan-
guage primarily with native speakers (Anglophones speak French
with Francophones, but not with fellow Anglophones and vice
versa in the case of English-speaking Francophones). This
means that *within* each mother-tongue community the second language does not to an appreciable extent really serve a communicative function. That function is reserved for contact *between*
groups.
    It can be seen that these bilinguals differ in important
respects from certain other groups that have been investigated.

For example, in Fishman's (Fishman, Cooper, & Ma, 1971) study
of Puerto Rican immigrants in New York, the Spanish-English bilinguals to all intents and purposes possessed approximately
the same level of skill in their second language. Bilingualism was the rule in that community, not the exception. The
second language also served a communicative function within the
home-speech community and Spanish speakers would, in certain
circumstances, use English rather than Spanish among themselves.
    The Quebec populations we are dealing with also differ
from bilinguals in many countries that were once colonies and
where the second language is that of the former rulers. An
example that comes to mind is the population of second-language
speakers of English in the Philippines. Unlike the situation
in Quebec, in the Philippines English has a communicative function within the home community. It is also rarely used with
native speakers since they are so few in number. It is clear
then that any comparisons one may wish to make between our
studies and others must take into account certain important
ways various multilingual societies can differ.

SHARED SPEECH CODE

    One problem we are confronted with in answering the ques-
tion of whether the different patterns of speech exhibited by
a population of second-language users actually constitute the
shared code of a speech community is that of variability.
There may be a great deal of variation between individuals'
mastery of the second language, and consequently speech patterns may differ radically between the highly and the poorly
skilled. Moreover, individuals who are not highly practiced
with the language may show considerable variation from one occasion to the next in the way they speak. The problem of view-
ing the speech of a second-language-speaking population as a
community code thus becomes one of finding a way to handle the
great variation in speech patterns, and this would appear to
involve a consideration of the nature of second-language acquisition.
    In terms of language development, this problem of vari-
ability can be viewed as follows. Unskilled second-language
users will exhibit a great deal of nonnativelike elements and
structures in their speech. Moreover, they may do so in a
variable way, sometimes employing the nativelike variant of a
target language element, sometimes not. As skill with the language progresses, nativelike elements will be included to a
greater degree in the speech and more and more nonnativelike
elements will be eliminated. An important developmental question, then, is whether the elimination of certain elements and
introduction of new ones proceeds in a systematic fashion or

in a random manner. For example, does mastery of English voiced *th* simply involve overall increases in its appearance where appropriate with the corresponding elimination of the nonnativelike variants of /ð/ or is there some patterned relationship between the way new elements are introduced and old ones eliminated?

Linguists have developed various methods for describing and analyzing the variation one encounters in first-language speech (Bickerton, 1971; Cedergren & Sankoff, 1974; Labov, 1969; Sankoff, 1974). Gatbonton (1975) employed a method derived from the work of Bickerton (1971, 1973a, & 1973b) that appears to hold some promise for the study of second-language speech variability at the phonological level. The paradigm of Bickerton (1971) was originally developed for handling speech variation related to historical changes across generations of speakers. It seemed reasonable therefore, to suppose that it might prove useful in handling speech variability related to the kinds of changes that can occur across time within a single individual. (We do not intend here to imply any direct connection between mechanisms underlying historical change and those involved in language development in the individual, although the question about whether there may be similarities in the two processes is itself an interesting one.)

In the approach used by Gatbonton (1975) the speech of a second-language speaker was viewed as consisting of both "correct" (nativelike) and "incorrect" (nonnativelike) pronunciations of target language sounds. The analysis consisted of identifying the linguistic environments where the correct and/or incorrect variants of target language sounds occurred and then determining whether the distribution of these variants was random or systematic across the environments. The following example may illustrate this approach.

For a given target sound, say voiceless *th* as in *three* and *thought,* a number of phonetic environments can be specified where the target variable (here: /θ/) can occur. For example, the target can occur between vowels (*ether*), in a cluster (*three*), or initially before a vowel (*thought*). From a sample of an individual's second-language speech one might find some environment, A, in which the speaker always used the correct variant of the target, while in environment B both correct and incorrect variants occurred, and so on. In this way it is possible to characterize the distribution of correct and incorrect variants across a set of environments.

The descriptive model used by Gatbonton (1975) to handle this type of phonetic variability specifies, for a given target variable that is to be mastered, a set of stages through which learners pass in moving from the least nativelike stages of mastery of the language to the most nativelike stage. This model is shown in Table 1. The column headings list the rele-

TABLE 1

Model of the Distribution of Correct (C) and Incorrect (I)
Pronunciation of a Target Language Variant as a Function of
Level of Second-Language Development

Level of development[a]	Phonetic environments			
	A	B	C	D
1	*I*	*I*	*I*	*I*
2	*IC*	*I*	*I*	*I*
3	*IC*	*IC*	*I*	*I*
4	*IC*	*IC*	*IC*	*I*
5	*IC*	*IC*	*IC*	*IC*
6	*C*	*IC*	*IC*	*IC*
7	*C*	*C*	*IC*	*IC*
8	*C*	*C*	*C*	*IC*
9	*C*	*C*	*C*	*C*

[a] Numbers indicate increasingly advanced level of second language mastery.

vant environments, ordered in the sequence according to which correct variants tend to be most frequently found. As presented in Gatbonton (1975) these environments are spedified in terms of distinctive features. The rows designate developmental levels. The cell entries specify whether correct (*C*) variants, incorrect variants (*I*), or both (*IC*) are used in that environment by speakers of a particular stage of development. As can be seen from the table, the model involves the gradual spread of *C* variants in an orderly manner across the environments and then elimination of the co-occurring *I* elements in the same orderly manner. Note that if the occurrence of *C* and *I* elements were random and language acquisition only involved the gradual reduction in the overall numbers of *I* elements, then the patterns one could expect to see would number 81 (= 3^4) instead of 9 as shown in the table.

The subjects in Gatbonton's (1975) study were 27 French-Canadian males who spoke English with varying degrees of proficiency. Tape recordings were made of these speakers reading

two English diagnostic paragraphs and conversing with an English speaker. The sounds that were analyzed were the nativelike and nonnativelike variants of the voiced interdental fricative /ð/, the voiceless interdental fricative /θ/, and the
velar glide /h/. The main finding pertinent to the present
discussion was that for each of the three phonological variables, the informants exhibited distributions of nativelike
and nonnativelike variants of the target sounds conforming in
a statistically significant manner to the patterns shown in
Table 1. By way of example, Table 2 shows the empirically con-
structed matrix for performance with /ð/ on the reading task.
These findings suggest that there is a systematic pattern according to which new sounds are introduced into the second-language user's repertoire and old elements are eliminated.

The analysis just described assigned speakers to different levels in the acquisition process according to the distribution of the variables of a given target sound. To validate
this part of the analysis Gatbonton(1975) played the recordings of the 27 speakers to 11 Anglophones who rated them on
nine-point scales ranging from "very poor" speakers of English
to "very fluent." The rankings of the speakers obtained in
this way from Anglophone judges correlated .80 or better with
the rankings assigned by the linguistic analysis, supporting
the notion that the different distributional patterns of sounds
do correspond to developmental levels.

Any of a number of different factors may be responsible
for this systematicity in development: perceptual and articu-
latory factors, factors deriving from linguistic interference,
perhaps even cognitive factors related to the learner's construction of an interlanguage. What is important for the present discussion is that it appears possible to describe some of
the speech patterns of a second language using population in a
way that includes the speech of all members of that group regardless of their level of proficiency and that relates linguistic variation to language development in a systematic way.
Of special interest is the further finding reported in Gatbonton (1975) that some of these patterns may have social significance. For example, for the target variables /ð/ and /θ/
but not /h/, speakers' levels of development as determined by
this method were statistically related to their feelings of
ethnic identification (feelings of being Quebecois as opposed
to Canadian). Speakers with patterns nearer the nativelike
end of the matrix were significantly less nationalistic than
those with patterns corresponding to earlier phases. There
were no such differences for /h/. Thus, it appears that some
features of speech (namely, /ð/ and /θ/) may matter more than
others; that is, they may carry the symbolic load of signaling
ethnic group affiliation more heavily than do other features.
There was, incidentally, no relation between overall fluency

(overall proportion of nativelike to nonnativelike elements in speech) and nationalistic feelings. In some respects, then, the findings parallel those of Labov (1963) who found that speakers with greater centralization of certain vowels in their mother tongue English had different feelings of group identification from those with less centralization. The present findings with bilinguals are, of course, quite consistent with the fact that in Quebec there exist strong feelings about language and ethnic loyalty.

TABLE 2

Distribution of the Nativelike (C) and Nonnativelike (I) Variants of /ð/ in the Reading Speech of the 27 Informants

Informants	Phonetic Environments[a]				
	A $\begin{bmatrix} +voc \\ -cns \end{bmatrix}$ ##_	B $\begin{bmatrix} +cns \\ +voice \\ +cont \end{bmatrix}$ ##_	C $\begin{bmatrix} +cns \\ +voice \\ -cont \end{bmatrix}$ ##_	D $\begin{bmatrix} +cns \\ -voice \\ +cont \end{bmatrix}$ ##_	E $\begin{bmatrix} +cns \\ -voice \\ -cont \end{bmatrix}$ ##_
1, 17	I	I	I	I	I
	I	I	I	IC*	I
,10,12,13 5,16,19	IC	I	I	I	I
,18	IC	I	IC*	I	I
,6,29	IC	IC	I	I	I
	IC	IC	I	I	IC*
,28	IC	IC	IC	IC	I
	IC	IC	IC	C*	I
	IC	IC	IC	I	IC*
4	IC	IC	IC	IC	IC
4,22 5,27	C	IC	IC	IC	IC
1	C	C	IC	IC	IC
6	C	C	C	IC	IC

Starred items indicate entries that deviated from expected patterns.

These results suggest that one might be able to regard the heterogeneous speech patterns of a second language using population as reflecting a common speech code. This seems possible because of the connections that appear to exist between different stages in the acquisition process. Further work will have to specify in more detail the nature of the transitions from one stage to the next and deal more directly with the underlying mechanisms.

SOCIOLINGUISTIC RULES OF SPEECH

Every speech community has rules concerning how one ought to speak about certain topics in particular situations in a way that shows respect, friendliness, anger, and so on (Fishman, 1972; Hymes, 1971). In the context of bilingual societies, researchers have observed how people switch between languages as a function of topic and situation much as monolinguals switch between styles (Fishman et al., 1971). The few studies that have examined nonfluent bilinguals explicitly in this regard have explored psychological factors governing language choice between bilinguals who have different mother tongues. A related topic that has received attention in the literature is that of speech style accommodation where different languages or regional varieties of a language are involved (Bourhis, Giles, & Lambert, 1975; Giles, Taylor, & Bourhis, 1973).

In the present case we were interested in the reactions of nonfluent second-language users who generally use their second language with native speakers in a variety of situations. For example, many Montreal Anglophones have to use French with Francophones in order to obtain information over the telephone, in short interchanges with shop clerks, in casual conversation with strangers on buses, and so on. In some of these situations native speakers would naturally use a more formal style of speaking while in others a casual style would be more appropriate. Many nonfluent users of French, however, do not have control over different speech styles in the language and are consequently unable to vary their manner of speaking in a way that is appropriate for the situation. How then, do such speakers handle a situation which requires a speech style outside their competence? Segalowitz (1976) attempted to explore this question with the following experiment.

Anglophone subjects with only an intermediate level of competence in French were asked to communicate twice in French with an unseen Francophone interlocutor and, for purposes of comparison, twice in English with an unseen Anglophone. The experiment was arranged so that on one occasion with each interlocutor there were implicit cues making a relatively formal or careful speech style the appropriate one while a casual speech style was appropriate on the other occasion. An exchange between subject and interlocutor consisted of the interlocutor speaking first on an assigned topic and then the subject speaking on the same topic. In reality, there were no interlocutors present and the subjects heard only prerecorded tapes of confederates. Following each of the four exchanges, the subjects answered a rating scale questionnaire concerning how they felt while speaking, what general impression of the interlocutor they obtained from hearing him speak, and what impressions about themselves they believed they conveyed to the interlocutor. A control group listened to the interlocutors without speaking. It was hypothesized that the Anglophone subjects would show considerable discomfort in the use of casual French conversations compared to the careful condition since the speech style in which they were most skilled (formal classroom register) was more similar to a native speaker's careful style then to his casual style. No such difference was predicted for the mother-tongue (English) condition. It was also hypothesized that the subjects would handle their discomfort in the casual speech condition by downgrading the personality of the interlocutor and believing that the interlocutor formed a bad impression of them. This prediction was derived from a consideration of Bem's (1972) self-perception theory. In terms of the present experiment, it was hypothesized that subjects would have some awareness that they were not speaking in an appropriately friendly and casual manner, and would conclude that they therefore really did not like the interlocutor after all.

The results supported these predictions. Experimental subjects reported feeling most ill at ease in the casual French condition. Moreover, in the casual French condition the experimental subjects attributed more negative personality characteristics to their interlocutor than they did in the careful speech condition whereas this difference vanished when they used their native English. On the other hand, control subjects reacted more positively in the casual condition than in the careful condition in both languages. In addition, experimental subjects believed they appeared less friendly when using their second language than when using their native language. They also believed they appeared significantly less intelligent and less self-confident in the casual condition than in the careful condition when speaking French but believed the reverse when speaking English. They claimed it was easier to express themselves and that they were better understood in the casual condition than in the careful condition in English but the reverse when using French.

These findings have certain implications for second-language learners who have only mastered basic vocabulary and syntax in their new language but have not developed skills in the domain of linguistic variability. Such people may find social interactions with native speakers in their second language to be a relatively negative experience and may become discouraged from pursuing language practice with native speakers. This could be socially unproductive in societies attempting to promote a majority language among members whose native tongue is a minority one.

It will be important in future research to further investigate the way the social perceptions of nonfluent speakers are affected by the types of encounters they have with native speakers. Depending on their reactions, they may avoid certain speech situations and seek out others. This may in turn affect the course of the individual's language development by placing constraints on how far development proceeds and by influencing the selection of patterns the learner is exposed to and ultimately incorporates in his speech. What we may find, then, is that there is a complex interaction between the sociolinguistic requirements of communication, the social cognitions the individual develops when communicating, and the speech patterns the individual ultimately exhibits in his second-language speech.

SHARED ATTITUDES

The final issue we have explored is the sharing of attitudes about what it means to speak in a particular way. Investigations of this in mother-tongue communities (e.g., Labov, 1970) have shown that sometimes the way a person speaks is interpreted by listeners as indicating something about the speaker's feelings or beliefs. Such community beliefs about the social significance of one's way of speaking could, in principle, provide the basis on which social forces may exert an influence on individuals' speech patterns. For example, if certain speech patterns are believed to reflect pretentiousness or lack of identification with one's group, then it is likely that individuals exhibiting them would be treated relatively negatively by others in the group. Similarly, patterns that appear to indicate friendliness or group solidarity will be more positively received and encouraged.

In the bilingual context such pressures, if they exist, may be an important factor determining what speech patterns second-language learners will acquire. For example, learners may be encouraged to use nativelike patterns when the home group regards high levels of second-language mastery as prestigious and indicative of the speaker's superior intelligence and level of education. On the other hand, a community may frown upon mastery of a second language that is too nativelike if there is the belief that nativelike control of the language is associated with a weakening of identity with the home group

and a desire to integrate into the other group. Clearly both
these factors may be operative within the same community at the
same time.

Gatbonton (1975) conducted a study that explored whether
within a group of French-Canadian speakers of English, there
existed shared attitudes toward different ways of speaking English. She presented six tape-recorded stimulus voices to a
group of French-Canadian college students who themselves had
some knowledge of English. Two of the stimulus voices were
those of French Canadians reading a neutral passage in English
with an extremely heavy accent. Two were those of French Canadians with nativelike competence in English. The rest were
those of French Canadians who exhibited an intermediate level
of skill. The listeners indicated on rating-scale question-
naires their impressions about the speakers' beliefs on various political issues relevant to nationalism in Quebec, as well
as their own opinions on these issues. They were also asked
to indicate their willingness to select the stimulus speakers
for positions of leadership or membership in local organiza-
tions engaged in activities that either involved or did not involve contact with Anglophones. They also rated their own
skills in English.

The first finding of interest was that the French-Canadian
listeners showed a strong agreement in the way they perceived
the stimulus speakers. Heavily accented English was associated
with attitudes that were highly pro-Francophone and not at all
pro-Anglophone. Beliefs that were very pro-Anglophone but not
pro-Francophone were attributed to speakers with nativelike
competence. The intermediate level speakers received mixed
ratings. What was interesting was that neither the listeners'
own feelings of nationalism nor their own abilities in English
were factors determining these perceptions. The listeners appeared to share as a group beliefs about the relationship between English-language fluency level and political attitudes.
(Incidentally, these beliefs did *not* in fact correspond to reality. The speakers who made the stimulus tapes also filled
out a rating-scale questionnaire, and no relationship was found
between their degree of nationalism and levels of fluency in
English.)

The listeners' own beliefs did, however, influence how
they claimed they would behave toward the speakers. Listeners
who were not themselves very nationalistic expressed the greatest willingness to choose the nativelike speakers for leadership and membership roles, regardless of the nature of the situation. Nationalistic listeners, on the other hand, did not
favor nativelike English ability if it was not absolutely an
asset to the situation. Thus, these listeners preferred to
choose speakers with lower levels of ability in English, over
those with nativelike fluency, for leadership and membership

roles in situations where no direct contact with Anglophones
was involved.

In one sense these results present another side of the
story relating integrative motivations to high levels of fluency (Gardner & Lambert, 1972). Here the community has judged
speakers to have high integrative motivations because they displayed high levels of fluency. More generally, what the results suggest is that social pressures may exist within the
home community that make some second-language speech patterns
more favored than others. Further research would have to explore the details of this relationship between the second-language user's accent and his group's reactions to him. It is
possible, as was indicated earlier, that some linguistic features may be more relevant to this relationship than others.
It is also possible that some bilinguals would shift their way
of speaking (change their second-language "register") depending on who is listening, what impression they wished to convey,
and so on.

CONCLUSIONS

We regard these studies as representing only a very modest
beginning to what will necessarily turn out to be a long and
complex program of research. Much further work remains to be
done in relating factors of ethnic identification to speech
variables and in understanding the way social cognitions are
formed in the context of second-language communication. These
social and psychological factors may be strongly implicated in
the shaping of the course of second-language development. We
are, however, extremely encouraged by the data we have obtained in these studies. They suggest to us that the second-language speech patterns of nonfluent speakers may be as amenable
to systematic analysis as is mother-tongue speech.

REFERENCES

Bem, D. Self-perception theory. In L. Berkowitz (Ed.),
    Advances in experimental social psychology (Vol. 6).
    New York: Academic Press, 1972.
Bickerton, D. Inherent variability and variable rules.
    Foundations of Language, 1971, 7, 457-492.
Bickerton, D. Quantitative vs. dynamic paradigm: the case
    of Montreal "Que." In C.J. Bailey & R.W. Shuy (Eds.),
    New ways of analyzing variations in English. Washington,
    D.C.: Georgetown University Press, 1973. (a)
Bickerton, D. The nature of the creole continuum. *Language*,
    1973, 49, 640-669. (b)

Bourhis, R., Giles, H., & Lambert, W.E.   Social consequences
    of accommodating one's style of speech: a cross national
    investigation. *International Journal of the Sociology of
    Language*, 1975, *6*, 55-72.
Cedergren, H., & Sankoff, D.   Variable rules: performance as
    a statistical reflection of competence. *Language*, 1974,
    50, 333-335.
Fishman, J.   Domains and the relationship between micro- and
    macro-sociolinguistics. In J. Gumperz and D. Hymes (Eds.),
    *Directions in sociolinguistics: The ethnography of com-
    munication*. New York: Holt, Rinehart & Winston, 1972.
Fishman, J., Cooper, R., Ma, R., et al.   *Bilingualism in the
    Barrio*. Bloomington, Ind.: Indiana University Press,
    1971.
Gardner, R., & Lambert, W.E.   *Attitudes and motivation in
    second language learning*. Rowley, Mass.: Newbury House,
    1972.
Gatbonton, E.   Systematic variations in second language
    speech: A sociolinguistic study. Unpublished doctoral
    dissertation, McGill University, 1975.
Giles, H., Taylor, D., & Bourhis, R.   Interpersonal accommo-
    dation through language: A Canadian example. *Language
    and Society*, 1973, *2*, 177-192.
Gumperz, J.   Sociolinguistics and communication in small
    groups. In J.B. Pride & J. Holmes (Eds.), *Sociolinguis-
    tics*. Harmondsworth, England: Penguin Books, 1972.
Labov, W.   The social motivation of sound change. *Word*,
    1963, *19*, 273-309.
Labov, W.   Contraction, deletion and inherent variability
    of the English copula. *Language*, 1969, *45*, 715-762.
Labov, W.   The study of language in its social context.
    Studium Generale, 1970. Also in J. Fishman (Ed.),
    Advances in the sociology of language. The Hague:
    Mouton, 1971.
Sankoff, G.   A quantitative paradigm for the study of com-
    municative competence. In R. Bauman & J. Sherzer (Eds.),
    Explorations in the ethnography of speaking. London:
    Cambridge University Press, 1974.
Segalowitz, N.   Communicative incompetence and the non-fluent
    bilingual. *Canadian Journal of Behavioural Science*,
    1976, *8*, 122-131.

Chapter 7

Norm and Deviation in
Bilingual Communities

EINAR HAUGEN

Harvard University

The concept of "norm" in reference to language is highly
ambiguous and slippery. It may refer to a standardized language like French, codified in grammars and sanctified by an
Academy, taught in schools, and written by authors, but spoken
by no one, except under duress. Any deviation from such a norm
is deemed to reveal one's lack of a proper education, and is
regarded as barbarism if it is unintentional. But it may be
acceptable if it is an intentional stylistic variation, either
as a mockery of the lower classes or as a relaxation of stand-
ards, a kind of "old shoe." I shall call this type of norm a
"rhetorical norm," since it has been the ideal of rhetoricians
and their grammatical henchmen for lo these many centuries.
Scientific linguists have generally rejected it, at least in
theory, and have proclaimed that it is their task to *de*scribe
not to *pre*scribe linguistic norms (Haugen, 1966, p. 51).

In bilingual communities some reflections of the rhetorical norm are preserved in the scorn expressed by educated writers for the deviations of daily speech from the official norms
of each language. I have recently found a new and instructive
specimen for my herbarium of bilingual abuse. In the year 1881
two rival editors of Norwegian-language newspapers in Minneapolis engaged in a rather vitriolic discussion about language.
They were both university-trained men of well-known urban families, immigrants from Norway within the decade, still in their
thirties, and editing secular weeklies for their countrymen
(Luth Jæger, 1851-1925, editor of *Budstikken*; Professor Sven
Oftedal, 1844-1911, editor of *Folkebladet*). One of them (Oftedal) was a clergyman, the other (Jæger) anticlerical, so they
had other things than language to feud about; but over some

months of the year 1881 this was their topic.

Curiously enough, the anticlerical editor was the one who upheld the rhetorical norm. He severely castigated the cleric for his "bad" Norwegian, in particular for interlarding some of his articles with English terms, more or less assimilated. When the cleric replied that he wrote as he did in order to be understood by his readers, our anticleric retorted that as a pastor and a professor of theology he had a responsibility to the growing generations to give them models of the "best possible Norwegian." As an editor he was also a teacher, "with the duty of maintaining the mother tongue and thereby also the desire to remain in touch with what is going on at home in the fatherland." With a touch of irony he continued that "it would be a different matter if Professor Oftedal could not help mixing and mistreating the language as he so often does in his paper, but his position as a professor forbids our believing that.... So it must be because he either does not wish to bother translating various English words and terms into Norwegian, does not have the time, does not want to, or thinks it is impressive to ornament his paper with these borrowed feathers and wishes to show that he knows a little more than his catechism, as the expression goes. We cannot know, of course, what the professor's real motivation is, but it must be one of these or all of them together" (*Budstikken*, Feb. 8, 1881).

If we consider his collection of incriminating examples, however, we are likely to find, as I did, that many if not all of the English terms are such as do not easily lend themselves to translation. They include words and expressions highly characteristic of American political and economic life, such as, "deadline," "pay as you go," "dark horse," "figures do not lie," "drawbacks," "a perjured villain," "common sense," "party vote," "logrolling," "filibustering." These are difficult to handle in any language except as loanwords. In the good pastor's text they are variously treated as integrated loans, but more often as switches, being set off by Roman type in an otherwise Gothic text or by quotation marks. Some of the abusive terms quoted from American politicians he has left in English, he says, "for decency's sake." His critic maintained that he could easily have replaced them by Norwegian words. But it is clear that our theologian had the feeling that most of his readers had learned about these things since their immigration and would therefore understand them best if one used the precise English words instead of some approximate equivalent in their mother tongue. He did so, of course, in full awareness of the patchwork result and the violation it constituted of the homeland rhetorical norm. That he still did it is especially interesting, since pastors were usually norm models for the standard language among the immigrants.

It is not my intention to go more deeply into an analysis

of this historical incident at this time.   I have reported it only to illustrate my main theme, the question of how and whether one can speak of a norm in a bilingual community.   One can document endlessly and in every immigrant group the often futile and partly misguided attempts to maintain the rhetorical norms of the homelands.   The ability to maintain any norms whatever of one's mother tongue in an environment where one nearly always hears and reads another requires continual vigilance, a vigilance I have described as "linguistic backbone." It also requires that one keep in constant touch with home base, i.e., that one have a chance to test one's competence against the developing and ever-changing norms of the homeland.   For immigrants this would have required either frequent travel to the homeland, which most of them could not afford, or extensive reading of its current literature, for which only a few had the taste.   At the very least it required that the speaker be in touch with a large body of monolinguals among his countrymen, but these would normally be exposed to the same influences as he.

Situations like these compel us to abandon the concept of the rhetorical norm in favor of one that I would think of as a "communicative norm."   This is one that takes into account the special situation of the bilingual speaker (and writer); and it is more like a spectrum, embracing the wide variation of situations in which the bilingual finds himself.   Our Norwegian cleric implicitly acknowledged the fact that his readers were also familiar with English, though perhaps imperfectly, since they still preferred to read their news in Norwegian.   He was therefore in all likelihood closer to those readers than our more academic editor.   In each immigrant community there have been intellectuals like our pastor, who have defended the use of English as a supplementary source of enrichment for the mother tongue.   I shall return to their comments in a moment.

The kind of communicative norm with which I am most familiar is that which assumes a relatively, but not absolutely, stable bilingual community.   Stable bilingual groups are less common among American immigrants than in some other parts of the world.   Our country has promoted a rapid tempo of assimilation through the American public school and the relative mildness of the segregation which immigrant groups have been permitted to maintain.   But one need only turn to India to find communities where different linguistic groups have been in contact for centuries without assimilating, i.e., giving up their distinct languages.   In this case a significant factor has been the caste system, which prevented what has been called "crossing over" through exogamy and personal friendships.   Even here the effects of language contact are visible to the close observer, as we see from a recent report by Nadkarni (1975) on a dialect of the Konkani language as spoken in the Indian state

of Karnataka. Konkani is an Indo-Aryan language spoken by a
relatively small, but self-important group living among a population of Kannada-speaking Dravidians. Even though they are
all fluent in Kannada, the Konkani refuse to accept it as their
own; but obviously without knowing it, they have adopted the
relative clause structure of Dravidian. Their Konkani has become a "bilingual dialect," or as I would now prefer to call
it, a "contact dialect" of their language. This means a dialect that differs from regional and social dialects by being
characteristic of bilingual speakers who incorporate features
from other dialects or languages. In this sense the English
spoken during the Norman-French domination of England was no
doubt to be characterized as a contact dialect of Anglo-Saxon,
a Franco-English which it might be appropriate, in modern jar-
gon, to call "Franglish."

As we have seen, those who cling categorically to the rhetorical norm either deride or deplore contact dialects and even
go so far as to deny that there is any norm whatever in their
usage. Like our normative editor, they hold that such infringe-
ments on the rhetorical norm, as they conceive it to be, are
due either to laziness, a moral defect, or to ignorance, an
intellectual defect, or to snobbery, a social defect. One
critic of midwestern Norwegian, a visitor from Norway, wrote:
"Strictly speaking, it is no language whatever, but a gruesome
mixture of Norwegian and English, and often one does not know
whether to take it humorously or seriously" (Haugen, 1953,
p. 57). In his recent volume on American Swedish, Nils Hasselmo (1974) provides us with a rich flora of similar comments by
Swedish observers of *their* countrymen in the period when Swedish immigration was still an active process. Their favorite
word for the language of the immigrants was "rotvalska," a
term used in Sweden to refer to a gypsy-related language spoken
by tramps and which we might translate roughly as "mishmash."
Thereupon the critics proceeded to lecture their emigrated
countrymen, if they took the language seriously; or they ridiculed them, if they took it humorously. In the latter case it
was a typical ploy to devise linguistic samples exaggerating
the English features usually leading to a distorted, cartoon-
like picture of how the immigrants actually spoke.

On the other hand, Hasselmo has also found that some Swedish commentators recognized the need and justification for a
wider spectrum of usage in an American bilingual community
(Hasselmo, 1974, p. 86). To this I can add the judgment of a
Norwegian-American pastor (not the one cited earlier), who
wrote in his memoirs that "mixing was not done to be affected,
but came so naturally that one simply does not notice it. Even
we pastors and others who might regard ourselves as 'cultured'
often fall into this sin of 'mixing'." He added, "When one
lives among these people and learns to understand the circum-

stances under which they live, one will forgive them" (Haugen, 1953, p. 58).

As anyone knows who has been following the literature in sociolinguistics, there is something familiar, perhaps even universal, about this situation and this conflict of views. On the one hand are those who either in the name of the cultural "Great Tradition" (as Fishman has called it) or in defense of language uniformity assert the maintenance of a rhetorical norm and condemn anything else as a barbarous deviation. On the other are those who defend deviation or cultural differences in language as rooted in specific circumstances of communication, a relativistic rather than a normative or absolutist view. A similar difference exists among linguists as well. The views of a Chomsky (1965, p. 3) that linguistics should deal "with an ideal speaker, in a completely homogeneous speech-community" stand against those of a Labov (1969) who operates with a variable competence, which is related to specific life situations and even to the life goals of its speakers.

When Labov (1969) defends the "logic of non-standard English," he is taking the same position vis-à-vis a deviant variety of English as the Swedish writer G.N. Malm toward American Swedish, when the latter asserted and defended in 1919 the existence and validity of a "Swedish-American" language. Malm advocated its use in literature and demonstrated by his own writings "how important it is, in describing Swedish-American types, to permit them in their dialogs to use their own, uncorrupted, often unjustly ridiculed everyday language" (Hasselmo, 1974, p. 91). Some would of course hold that even Black English is itself a contact dialect, with elements of African in its substratum. In any case the use of Black English, like the speaking of American Norwegian and American Swedish, gains one no power in the general community and is often associated with low-status groups. Status goes with power, and power engenders social pressure and prejudice, resulting in a downgrading of people because of their speech. Once we recognize that much of what passes as humor is a screen for antagonism and unjust discrimination, we will sympathize not only with the antidefamation league of the B'nai B'rith, but also with the American Polish League that is trying to stop the thoughtless use of Polish jokes in American television.

Let me now return to a consideration of what I have called the communicative norm of bilinguals. Certain views which I advanced on this topic in my basic study some twenty years ago have been under discussion in recent years, with some confirmation and some disconfirmation. Perhaps it is time to think it all through once more. To clarify this I shall ask your indulgence in a bit of reminiscence from the year 1960, when I was visiting Sweden. I had just been reading the last volume of Vilhelm Moberg's tetralogy about Swedish emigration and settle-

ment in Minnesota (Moberg, 1956). These novels have since been
translated into English and have been condensed into two mag-
nificent films, widely seen and praised in this country, entitled *The Emigrants* and *Unto a Good Land*. What cannot appear
either in the English translations or the films is Moberg's extensive use of American-Swedish dialog in the volumes that deal
with the settlement in Chisago County, north of Minneapolis, in
the 1850s. While in Sweden I read a critique of Moberg's use
of English words by a Swedish scholar who objected to them on
aesthetic grounds, perhaps we could say from the point of view
of Swedish rhetorical norms (Mjöberg, 1960). My own impression
as I read the novels was rather their improbability as realis-
tic examples of spoken American Swedish. In most writers this
would not have surprised me, but Moberg was a realist, and he
made something of a parade of his scholarly research into the
life of the Swedes in America. It puzzled me that many of his
examples deviated from what I had heard from American Swedes,
not to speak of the American Norwegian that I knew from childhood and that I had studied in the field in several midwestern
states.

The result was an article I published in a Swedish news-
paper, rashly attacking Moberg's American Swedish as "unreal-
istic and improbable." I called it, with some journalistic ex-
aggeration, "a mishmash of absurdities piled one upon the other
without considering the daily practice of emigrated American
Swedes." It reminded me of the deliberately concocted humorous
samples, and I reacted strongly, perhaps over-defensively. My
article stirred up a hornet's nest and provoked Moberg (who was
then still very much alive) into angry and cutting replies. He
flung in my face the charge that knowledge of American Norwegian did not qualify me to judge his American Swedish of the
1850s. He further accused me, quite rightly, of not having
studied the documents at his disposal when he wrote the novels.
He referred to letters and diaries he had read over the years,
above all the diary of one Andrew Peterson, a farmer in Minnesota. Peterson had started his diary in 1854 and kept it up
until his death some time in the 1890s. Moberg gleefully pointed out that this was available for inspection at the Minnesota
Historical Society in St. Paul (Haugen, 1960; Moberg, 1960).

After my return to Wisconsin in the fall of 1960 I made a
special pilgrimage to St. Paul to study the Peterson diary.
Of course my suspicions were verified. Not only were many of
Moberg's notations erroneous, but Peterson nowhere exhibited
the kinds of phrases used in Moberg's novels. Only one single
word to which I had objected proved to be a part of his language, the expression "speak meeting." It has since turned
out that Peterson was an ardent Baptist, and that these Swedish Baptists held "testimonial meetings" which they called
"speak meetings." So this curious word, which I have not been

able to find in any dictionary of American English, entered into his American Swedish, quite naturally, just as the word
"meeting" entered into that of non-Lutheran American Norwegians
whom I had studied.   One of my criticisms of Moberg concerned
the fact that his bibliography did not include the only scholarly study made of the Swedish of Chisago County, namely the
one by Professor Walter Johnson of the University of Washington,
who had grown up in the community and was thoroughly familiar
with its dialect (Johnson, 1942).   Moberg brushed aside my criticism, but Johnson later pointed out in a new article that
studying diaries and letters is a poor substitute for listening to the living speech of the present-day community, an opportunity which Moberg had but did not seize.   Johnson supported my contention, writing that the speech of the pioneers "was
not a hodgepodge, an indiscriminate mixing of American and
smålåndska phonetic and structural patterns" (Johnson, 1971,
p. 3).   He showed in some detail how many of Moberg's angli-
cisms were not part of general usage in the community.

In reporting this discussion I do not wish to raise again
the issue of Moberg's realism in reporting the American Swedish
of the 1850s.   I have nothing but admiration and respect for
the literary qualities of his work; my quarrel is only with his
failure to recognize the existence of a bilingual norm.   In a
way one can say that we were arguing past one another.   While
I expected a realist to follow the average norm, he felt no
qualms about including the more bizarre materials from a wider
spectrum of bilingual usage.   He was reaching out into what
Hasselmo (1974) has called "pathological switching," to some
extent characterizing the most anglicized and least educated
members of the community.

My rules for the norm included the principle that form
words are seldom borrowed, words like "how" and "as" in the expressions "how många" (for "how many") or "as du förstår" (for
"as you understand") (Moberg, 1956, pp. 32-34).   Another principle I had found was that cognates are rarely borrowed as
phonetic entities, but that they induce semantic transfer:
they are not loanwords, but loanshifts.   Yet Moberg (1956,
p. 53) wrote "Och nu vi go" for "And now we go," where natural
speech would have used the Swedish verb "gå."   A third rule is
that compounds such as "state church" and "Swedish made" would
either have been borrowed as units or retained as Swedish orig-
inals "statskörkan" and "svenskgjord" rather than have become
loanblends like Moberg's "statekörkan" and "svenskmakad."   Finally, I found that in most texts borrowings rarely run higher
than 5 to 10 percent of the running words, but they could be
much higher in some of his.

The basis for my rules was of course an intuition built
in through personal experience, but also statistics drawn from
my many interviews in the homes of Norwegian speakers in the
Midwest (Haugen, 1953, p. 61).   A norm can also be reflected

in the comments of informants on the language they speak and
what they hear from others within their communities. Even
though they admired the book norms exhibited by clergymen, they
did not approve of people from their own group who tried to
speak a "pure" Norwegian like that of the ministers. On the
other hand, they poked fun at those who adopted excessive numbers of English words, calling them "yankeefied" and holding
them to be "proud," "trying to be big shots," and the like.
Most people steered a middle course between these extremes, and
while professing a low opinion of their own dialects, an attitude reflecting their low status in the homeland, they went
right on using them into the second and third generation. In
doing so they created quite unconsciously a communicative norm
which anyone who has known their society will immediately recognize as genuine. In 1914 the Swedish-American writer Ernest
Skarstedt wrote that only two writers of fiction had succeeded
in "writing American Swedish absolutely correctly, i.e., get
in just those English words with just those distortions that
are really used by the common man." He criticized writers who
had created pseudo-sentences like "Jag tror inte, hon *regretted
it*" ["I don't think she regretted it"] or "Om vi inte råkas nu
hår *on earth*" ["If we don't meet now here on earth"] (Hasselmo,
1974, p. 101; quotation from 1914).

Even so we have to recognize that the communicative norm
which grows up in bilingual communities is more elastic and
less predictable than that of a monolingual community. Speakers have dual competence and can in principle draw on either
one at any time. The resources of both languages are available
to them, and only a vigorous effort enables the speakers to
keep them wholly apart. I have described the identification of
language membership as "tagging": when a rule or an item is
learned, it bears a tag that tells the speaker to which language it belongs. But by constant use in identical or similar
contexts, the tags fall off. It is clearly inefficient to maintain two systems in addressing the same speech partners. A
linguistic "tag" is one form of what linguists call "co-occur-
rence restrictions," though this is a somewhat wider concept.
If all the tags fall off, we could genuinely speak of a single
competence comprising both languages and their grammars; but in
spite of arguments to this effect, I am not prepared to buy the
idea, except in the case of pidgins and creole languages. Certainly the trend to merger is present in any bilingual community. But it is usually one-sided: the mother tongue suffers
under the impact of a dominant other tongue that is forced upon speakers by the power relations of the community. A language which has official or majority status with many monolingual speakers turns the weaker, minority language into a contact dialect, if it does not completely eliminate the latter by
acculturating and eventually assimilating its speakers.

In his discussion of the bilingual norm Hasselmo (1974) has developed a theory of borrowing which he calls "ordered selection." He regards the dual competence of the speakers as one that in principle makes all English and all Swedish forms available to the speaker of American Swedish. But in performance the speaker is restricted by the speech situation in making his choices. In specifying this process, he assumes five levels or layers of choice: lexemes, derivative suffixes, morphological suffixes, form words, and prosody, in this order. If a speaker chooses a native form on any one of these levels, this blocks the choice of English forms on the later levels. So, having decided to say "the tough guys," the speaker who chooses to use the Swedish plural suffix -ar on the noun, is then forced to use Swedish grammar for the rest of the phrase, producing "de tough-a guy-ar-na," and is blocked from saying "the tough guy-ar." But if he chooses to use an English plural, "guys," he can make it grammatical American Swedish by saying "de tough-a guy-s-en," but is blocked from saying "the tough-a guys." In effect this is a way of restating more precisely the generally accepted rule that bound forms are not borrowed independently of the free forms with which they occur. Within this linguistically determined competence model he grants that the options are strongly limited by traditional preferences, i.e., that some words are normally chosen in their English form, others in their native forms and that some are normally given English affixes, others native ones. After developing this model, Hasselmo has investigated the acceptability of the choices made, using as his informants American-Swedish speakers from the very community of Moberg's immigrants, Chisago County. He found, as I had in similar American-Norwegian communities, a high degree of stabilization of the borrowed lexicon, with little difference from the first to the third generation (Hasselmo, 1974).

Criticism of Hasselmo's views (and by implication, of my views) concerning a bilingual norm has been offered by Sture Ureland in recent publications (Ureland, 1975). Ureland's field work was chiefly among residual speakers of Swedish in Texas (Ureland, 1971, 1972). While giving Hasselmo's work its due praise, he rejects his theoretical model of ordered selection: "To the present writer such normative statements regarding the acceptability or grammaticality of certain structures should not be the task of a bilingual study. The sociolinguistic situation of American Swedish is not of such a nature that it allows for categorical rule statements" (Ureland, 1975, p. 10). Ureland instances the many examples of the borrowing of suffixes and form categories across language borders without corresponding borrowing of loanword stems, by way of bilingual speakers. By Hasselmo's theory these bilinguals must therefore have produced "ungrammatical" forms before these could enter the other language. He attributes Hasselmo's attempts (and by implication mine) to find bilingual norms to our period of "structuralism" (which now of course is a dirty word), before we had learned about the possibilities of "variable competence" (Haugen, 1972, p. 321).

A similar critique of Hasselmo's theory has been offered by two Danish collectors of American Danish, Kjaer and Baumann-Larsen (1974). Their counterexamples reflect what I would describe as completely "ungrammatical" speech compared to that of settled groups of Danish Americans in rural areas. There are sentences in their recorded material such as "*I* levede" ("I lived") and "*I will never care for* at have så *much* land" (Kjaer and Baumann-Larsen, 1974, p. 425). It is significant that the samples presented were collected from persons past eighty years of age. The authors rightly reject the theory that their informants were aphasics, but I would suggest that they could surely be described as amnesic. After having spoken nothing but English for many years, perhaps decades, even with other Danes, they are suddenly faced by eager young scholars from Denmark, who ask them to speak a half-forgotten language into their microphones. They are residual speakers with a vengeance, who can not help their constant code shifts, even within syntactic units, contrary to the norms in communities that have learned to live with two languages and have sorted them out into reasonably consistent patterns of speech.

Without reference to either of the Swedish or Danish critiques here cited, I had already accepted and developed the concept of "approximative norms" launched by Nemser (1969), though I prefer to call them "intermediate norms." In a 1970 study entitled "The Stigmata of Bilingualism" I granted that "in the world of the bilingual anything is possible, from virtually complete separation of the two codes to their virtual coalescence. The reasons for this are clearly rooted in the possibilities for variable competence in the human brain" (Haugen, 1972, p. 317). Ureland reminds us that as far back as 1949 Bazell wrote that "there are no limits to the morphological influence one language can have on another" (Bazell, 1949, p. 393). He neglects to add that Bazell went on to point out the differential resistance to influence by different parts of the system. But in my study of Norwegian in America in 1953 I wrote: "We may assume, as a basis for discussion, that bilingualism leads inevitably to a certain confusion of patterns" (Haugen, 1953, p. 10). I went on to demonstrate, as well as my material permitted, that within this complex world of bilingual living there was no occasion to scorn the norm of those who have created out of two languages a compromise, a communicative norm that tells them when it is necessary and appropriate to use a word from the second language. Just what this norm is depends on the factors I have suggested here.

While in one sense this norm may be intermediate, it has the
potentiality for stabilization and effective functioning in
new environments. This may be what occurred when that contact
dialect of Anglo-Saxon known as Middle English got rid of the
dominance of the Anglo-Norman nobility.
Finally, you may ask what bearing this discussion of norms
has on the problems of bilingual education. That is beyond the
scope of this chapter. But I may suggest that in any program
of bilingual education one needs to take into account the inevitable conflict between the rhetorical norms of the standard
languages and the actual communicative norms of the bilingual
communities. By this time there are numerous studies of code
switching, interference, and borrowing, all of which operate
to induce linguistic change among bilinguals. To resist such
phenomena with all one's might and main requires a rigid linguistic backbone. It may be better to bend than to break.
Acceptance of useful convergence between codes is better than
a total rejection of the mother tongue, which is likely to result if one always and everywhere insists on the rigid rhetorical norms of the academicians.

REFERENCES

Bazell, C.E. *Proceedings of the Sixth International Congress
    of Linguists*. Paris: Klincksieck, 1949.
Chomsky, N. *Aspects of the theory of syntax*. Cambridge:
    MIT Press, 1965.
Hasselmo, N. *Amerikasvenska. En bok om språkutvecklingen i
    Svensk-Amerika*. Stockholm: Esselte studium, 1974.
Haugen, E. *The Norwegian language in America: A study in
    bilingual behavior*. Philadelphia: University of Penn-
    sylvania Press, 1953 (2. ed., Bloomington: Indiana
    University Press, 1964).
Haugen, E. Vilhelm Mobergs amerikasvenska "sammelsurium av
    orimligheter." *Svenska Dagbladet*, May 11, 1960. Mobergs
    amerikasvenska — en replik. *Svenska Dagbladet*, June 3,
    1960. Andrew Petersons språk. *Svenska Dagbladet*, Decem-
    ber 2, 1960.
Haugen, E. Linguistics and language planning. In W. Bright
    (Ed.), *Sociolinguistics*. The Hague: Mouton, 1966.
    Pp. 50-71.
Haugen, E. The stigmata of bilingualism. In A.S. Dil (Ed.),
    The ecology of language. Stanford: Stanford University
    Press, 1972. Pp. 159-190.
Johnson, W. American loanwords in American Swedish. In H.
    Larsen & C.A. Williams (Eds.), *Scandinavian studies pre-
    sented to George T. Flom by colleagues and friends*.
    Urbana, Ill.: Univ. of Illinois Press, 1942. Pp. 79-91.

Johnson, W.   The recording of American Swedish. *Americana Norvegica,* 1971, *3,* 64-73.

Kjaer, I., & M. Baumann-Larsen.   'De messy ting.' In P. Andersen (Ed.), *Festskirift til Kristian Hald.* Copenhagen: Akademisk forlag, 1974. Pp. 421-430.

Labov, W.   The logic of nonstandard English. *Georgetown Monographs in Languages and Linguistics,* 1969, *22,* 1-45.

Mjöberg, J.   Nybyggarnas språk. *Svenska Dagbladet,* April 27, 1960.

Moberg, V.   *Nybyggarna.* Stockholm: Bonniers, 1956.

Moberg, V.   Utbandrarnas språk. *Svenska Dagbladet,* May 22, 1960. Utvandrarnas språk hos Vilhelm Moberg. *Svenska Dagbladet,* June 9, 1960. Utvandrarna vittnar om sitt språk. *Svenska Dagbladet,* December 23, 1960.

Nadkarni, M.V.   Bilingualism and syntactic change in Konkani. *Language,* 1975, *51,* 672-683.

Nemser, W.   Approximative systems of foreign language learners. *The Yugoslav Servo-Croatian-English Contrastive Project, Studies B.1.* Zagreb: Institute of Linguistics, 1969.

Ureland, P.S.   Report on Texas-Swedish research. *Svenska Landsmål och Svenskt Folkliv,* 1971, *295,* 27-74.

Ureland, P.S.   Observations in Texas-Swedish phonology. *Studia Linguistica,* 1972, *25,* 69-110.

Ureland, P.S.   Review of N. Hasselmo, *Amerikasvenska. Svenska Landsmål och Svenskt Folkliv,* 1975, *300.*

Chapter 8

English the World Over: A Factor in
the Creation of Bilingualism Today

JOSHUA A. FISHMAN   ROBERT L. COOPER   YEHUDIT ROSENBAUM

Yeshiva University   *Hebrew University*

The great world languages of today are languages of empire, past and present. Only two, Mandarin Chinese and Russian, continue as languages of administration within single,
ethnolinguistically diverse states. The others — Arabic, English, French, and Spanish — are imperial legacies, having survived the disintegration of the empires that fostered them.

THE SURVIVAL OF FORMER "POST IMPERIAL" LANGUAGES

Not all imperial languages survive within former colonial
territories. Brosnahan (1963) points out that the language of
Attila and his Huns vanished from Europe and that Turkish, the
language of administration and authority in the Middle East
for a thousand years, flowed back to Anatolia with the collapse
of the Ottoman empire. In commenting on the case of three languages that did survive the empires which introduced them —
Arabic, Greek, and Latin — Brosnahan isolated four features
that accompanied the imposition of these languages. First,
these languages spread with military conquest, becoming the
languages of imperial administration. Second, the military
authority which introduced them was maintained for several centuries, giving the languages time to take root. Third, these
languages spread in multilingual areas. A unified administration promoted commercial, religious, and political contacts
among linguistically diverse peoples, and the language of administration served as a lingua franca. Fourth, the spread of
these languages was marked by material advantages associated
with learning them. Knowledge of the imposed languages, if
not an absolute prerequisite for government employment, formal

103

education, or commercial activity, enhanced the speaker's opportunities in these fields. According to Brosnahan, the un-
successful imposition of the language of Attila and of Turkish
can be explained in terms of the absence of one or more of
these four features. Attila's language disappeared in Europe
because his empire dissolved too quickly for the language to
become firmly established there. Turkish vanished in part because of the linguistic homogeneity of much of the Ottoman empire and in part because knowledge of Turkish did not confer
material benefits on persons of non-Turkish origin. While the
European portions of the Ottoman empire were linguistically diverse, the Asian and African portion was united by Arabic,
which in addition to being already spoken over most of the
area, was the language of a high culture and a universal religion, one to which the conquerors themselves subscribed. In
the Arabic-speaking portions of the empire, Arabic was the language of administration at all but the highest levels of authority. Turkish was used at the top level of governmental administration, to which only Turks were admitted as members.
Except in the Turkish-speaking provinces, moreover, commerce
and finance were carried on largely in Arabic and Greek. Thus
the material advantages associated with learning Arabic, Greek,
and Latin, during the period of those languages' expansion,
were absent in the case of Turkish.

Subject populations probably adopted Arabic, Greek, and
Latin only for specialized purposes initially — for commerce,
finance, education, religion, law, or dealings with governmental authorities, and maintained their mother tongues for other
purposes. It is likely, in other words, that at first the conquerors' languages only partially displaced the indigenous languages and even then not for all sections of the population.
Eventually, however, in many portions of the original empires,
the imperial languages either pushed out the people speaking
indigenous languages or absorbed the indigenous languages completely, becoming adopted as mother tongues. For example, as
Brosnahan (1963, p. 13) points out with respect to the spread
of Arabic, that language absorbed all the other Semitic dialects of Arabia, completely displaced Coptic, and pushed Ber-
ber back into the desert, becoming the general language and in
most places the only language "of all the peoples from Aleppo
to Aden and from Oman to Morocco."

Of the other world languages of today which are no longer
the languages of unified empires but which are themselves imperial legacies — English, French, and Spanish — the last probably comes closest to Arabic in the degree to which it has
displaced indigenous languages as mother tongue. Spanish has
become the general mother tongue within the former Spanish empire in Central and South America. However, many of the Central and South American Indian languages have survived, al-

though usually in reduced circumstances, and exist side by side with Spanish, which has displaced them for some but not all purposes among substantial numbers of speakers.

English and French have also been adopted as mother tongues by indigenous peoples living within the territories of the former British, French, and Belgian empires, but such adoption has generally been the exception rather than the rule. One can point to some elite families in India, Indochina, and Africa which have adopted the imperial language as the language of the home (see, for example, Alexandre, 1971), but by and large where English and French are spoken by indigenous populations in former Anglophone and Francophone colonies, they are learned as additional languages and not spoken as mother tongues. English and French have been maintained as mother tongues by the descendants of colonial settlers, as in the United States and Canada, and have been acquired as mother tongues by the descendants of immigrants to such territories and by the descendants of persons forcibly removed to such territories. Although there are important exceptions, particularly with respect to North American Indian populations, when English and French are spoken as mother tongues within the territories of former colonies, they are spoken by the descendants of the displaced and not by the descendants of the original inhabitants. Unlike Spanish, the use of which as an additional language is confined principally to the territories originally conquered by Spain, the use of English and French is by no means limited to former colonial territories. Both languages are used throughout the world as additional languages.

Are the forces which promote the spread of a language as an additional language the same as those which promoted the spread of Arabic, Greek, and Latin as mother tongues? Although all are likely to promote the spread of a language as an additional language (after all, before a language can spread as a mother tongue it must first spread as an additional language), it seems clear that not all are prerequisites for such expansion. English and French, for example, are spoken as additional languages in countries which were never part of an Anglophone or a Francophone empire. No one would claim that military conquest is a prerequisite for bilingualism, whether the additional language is a world language or not. Within those countries which formerly were colonies, moreover, it is doubtful that the expansion of the imperial language as an additional language depended on the duration of military authority for several generations. It is plausible that less time is required for one language to supplant another partially, being employed for some of the functions for which the mother tongue was originally used, or for one language to be learned for entirely new functions which are introduced along with the language, than for one language to supplant another as mother

tongue. Duration of authority may be less important in determining whether an imperial language remains in a former colonial territory as an additional language than it is in determining whether the language spreads there as a mother tongue.

With respect to the four conditions — military imposition,
duration of authority, linguistic diversity, and material incentives, it is not clear what their independent contribution
is to the promotion of a language, whether as an additional
language or as a mother tongue. Territories formerly under imperial rule are, for example, more likely to be linguistically
diverse than other countries. If an imperial language has a
more important status in former colonies than in other countries, to what extent is the enhanced status a function of linguistic diversity and to what extent is it a function of the
forces, motivations, and interactions implied by former imperial rule? Besides asking what the independent contribution of
each of the four factors is, one can also ask what other factors promote the spread of a language as an additional language. This chapter summarizes the results of a study designed to answer such questions for English.

HYPOTHESES AS TO ADDITIONAL PROMOTIONAL FACTORS

What factors, besides those identified by Brosnahan, might
promote the spread of a language as an additional language?
Some of these factors, which are among those suggested in connection with the spread of Amharic (Cooper, 1975), are likely
to be urbanization, industrialization or economic development,
and educational development. In addition, we can suggest religious composition and world-power political affiliation.

URBANIZATION

Towns often serve as loci for the spread of an additional
language. A good example is Amharic, which appears to be
spreading out from Ethiopia's towns and from the roads connect-
ing them (Cooper and Horvath, 1973). For one thing, towns
tend to be more linguistically diverse than the surrounding
countryside. Persons from different linguistic areas create
linguistic diversity within the towns to which they migrate
and they must often use an additional language as a lingua
franca there. Second, governmental agencies tend to be con-
centrated in towns. People who do not speak natively the language of governmental administration may need to use an additional language when transacting government business. Third,
there are apt to be greater educational opportunities in towns,
particularly in developing countries. If the additional language is learned mainly in schools, urbanization would be re-

lated to its acquisition by the population. These factors can be seen at work in Kampala (Scotton, 1972), for example, where English is the official language and where it serves, with Swahili, as one of the two chief lingua francas. Learned only in school, it is employed as a lingua franca only by those who have stayed long enough in school to have learned it.

ECONOMIC DEVELOPMENT

Educational language policy, while often based on political considerations, is influenced by economic constraints. A language of wider communication sometimes serves as a medium of instruction if there are not enough teachers to teach via local languages or if textbooks and other teaching materials have not been developed in local languages. Teacher training and the development of teaching materials may be more expensive in the short run than the hiring of expatriate teachers and the use of texts written in languages of wider communication. The use of additional languages for other than educational purposes may also be determined by economic considerations. Languages of wider communication may be employed as technical languages, in manuals for the use and maintenance of equipment, for example, if local languages have not been developed for such uses. Local languages are less likely to be used for such purposes if the industrial work sphere is relatively unimportant, employing relatively few workers. Economic underdevelopment may also retard the work of language academies or other language planning agencies in modernizing local languages and in disseminating their recommendations. On the one hand, economic underdevelopment promotes reliance upon languages of wider communication for functions that might be fulfilled by local languages in more developed economies. On the other hand, economic development promotes the spread of languages of wider communication to the extent that the acquisition of such languages is school-dependent. Thus the direction of the relationship between economic development and the status of a language of wider communication is likely to depend on the criterion which is employed.

EDUCATIONAL DEVELOPMENT

To the extent that an additional language is learned primarily in school, the proportion of persons who know that language will be a function of educational opportunity. Since educational opportunity varies with economic development, it may seem unnecessary to posit educational development as another factor promoting the spread of an additional language. Its probable importance, however, makes it worth listing separately even if its independence as a predictor is open to question.

RELIGIOUS COMPOSITION

That economic advancement is not the only incentive for
learning an additional language can be seen in the case of Arabic, which is a classical language for educated persons throughout the Islamic world. As a language of revealed religion,
Arabic is perhaps unique among languages of wider communication. It is unlikely that one would learn English, French, or
Spanish for religious purposes inasmuch as sanctity is not
among the claims that can be made for those languages. Besides, Christian missionaries take pains to translate the Gos-
pels into local languages. On the other hand, in areas in
which universal religions or religions associated with high
cultures are not dominant, religious beliefs are likely to be
relatively particularistic, reflecting ethnic and linguistic
diversity, which in turn promotes the spread of lingua francas.
Such areas also tend to be underdeveloped economically and educationally. Thus religious composition may serve as a kind of
mediating variable with respect to the spread of English, to
which it may be related either via linguistic diversity or via
economic and educational development.

POLITICAL AFFILIATION

It is possible that a country's position vis-à-vis the
superpowers will be reflected in the languages taught as subjects and used as media of instruction in their schools and in
the languages used when dealing with foreign governments.
Thus Russian, for example, is more likely to be taught as a
subject of instruction in Eastern European schools than in
South American schools. It is of course not the political affiliation itself that promotes second-language acquisition but
rather the interactions which are encouraged or faciliated by
such affiliation, as, for example, in international trade.

INDEPENDENCE OF ADDITIONAL FACTORS

Economic and educational development are not the only suggested additional promotional factors which are related to one
another. All are related to one another. Economic development is related to urbanism, which in turn is related to educational development. Similarly, particularistic, folk religions are more likely to be dominant in countries which are
less economically developed. With respect to political affiliation, the third-world countries are in general less economically developed than countries which are firm allies of either
of the two great superpowers. Thus just as the independence
of Brosnahan's four factors as facilitators of language spread
is problematic, so too is the independence of the five addi-

tional factors that have been suggested here.

PROCEDURE

Information from secondary sources was gathered for each of 102 countries with respect to the position of English and with respect to various demographic, economic, educational, and other factors. In none of these countries was English the mother tongue of a substantial proportion of the population. These data were intercorrelated and then multiple regression analyses were performed on a number of criterion variables pertaining to the status of English.

CRITERION VARIABLES

The criterion variables employed were as follows.
1. The use of English as a medium of instruction in secondary schools. This information, obtained from Gage and Ohannessian (1974), was scored as follows for purposes of data analysis: 2 = used as a medium of instruction throughout the school system; 1 = used as a medium in some schools or in some classes; 0 = not used as a medium of instruction.
2. The use of English as a medium of instruction in primary schools. This information, obtained from Gage and Ohannessian, was scored in the same way as was the first criterion variable.
3. The use of English as a subject of instruction in secondary schools. This information, also obtained from Gage and Ohannessian (1974), was scored as follows: 2 = taught as a subject of instruction throughout the school system; 1 = taught in some schools or in some classes; 0 = not taught as a subject of instruction.
4. The use of English as a subject of instruction in primary schools. This information, obtained from Gage and Ohannessian, was scored as in the third criterion variable.
5. The percentage of the population enrolled in English classes in primary and secondary schools. The number of students enrolled in English classes (whether as subject or medium) at the primary and secondary school levels in each country, as estimated by Gage and Ohannessian, was divided by the total population for that country as reported in the *World Data Handbook* of the U.S. Government (1972).
6. A composite score based on 14 items with respect to the status of English. The components of this score were the five items previously described as well as the following: the use of English as an official language; the use of English as a language of governmental administration; the use of English as a lingua franca within the country; the use of English as a

technical language; the use of English as the first foreign language for most students; the use of English in universities; the proportion of daily newspapers published in English; the use of English on the radio; and the use of English on television. These variables were converted to standard scores to equalize their weight in the composite. The composite was computed by summing the standard scores and dividing by the number of variables for which there was information. Averages were employed because there were no countries for which information could be obtained on all variables. The number of countries for which each of these components was obtained and the correlation of each component with the composite variable are presented in Table 1. It can be seen that the components with the

TABLE 1

Correlations between the Composite Criterion and Each of Its Components (All Countries)

Component	Number of countries	Correlation with composite
Official status	94	.89
Language of government administration	102	.87
Lingua franca within country	88	.43
Technical language	49	.66
First foreign language studied by most students	102	.63
Use in universities	32	.80
Percent of daily newspapers in English	96	.84
Use on radio	80	.62
Use on television	38	.81
Medium of instruction, secondary schools	88	.87
Medium of instruction, primary schools	88	.75
Subject of instruction, secondary schools	88	.50
Subject of instruction, primary schools	88	.79
Percent of population in primary and secondary school English classes	87	.65

highest relationship to the composite were official status
(r = .89), use as a language of administration (r = .87), and
use as a medium of instruction in secondary school (r = .87).
The components with the lowest correlation to the composite
criterion were use as a lingua franca within the country
(r = .43), use as a subject of instruction in secondary school
(r = .50), and the use of English on the radio (r = .62). The
median correlation of the components with the composite was
.77.

The intercorrelations among the six criterion variables
are presented in Table 2. These coefficients ranged between
.21 and .87, with the median at .61. Thus these criteria appear independent enough to justify separate treatment.

TABLE 2

Intercorrelations among Criterion Variables (All Countries)

Criterion	Coefficient					
	1	2	3	4	5	6
1. Medium in secondary schools	—	.79	.33	.76	.58	.87
2. Medium in primary schools		—	.27	.69	.40	.75
3. Subject in secondary schools			—	.27	.21	.50
4. Subject in primary schools				—	.61	.79
5. Percentage population in English classes					—	.65
6. Composite						—

PREDICTOR VARIABLES

The variables chosen to represent the four conditions described by Brosnahan for Arabic, Greek, and Latin and the five
conditions we have suggested as possible contributors to the
spread of an additional language are as follows:
1. Military imposition. While not all colonies were obtained through military conquest, the use of force is a common
enough feature to justify former colonial status as an indi-
cator of former military imposition. Thus all countries were
classified as to whether or not they had been former Anglophone colonies.
2. Duration of military authority. This variable was
measured indirectly and inversely as recency of independence.
The decade in which independence was achieved was scored, with

all decades prior to 1801-1810 scored as zero, with that decade scored as one, and with subsequent decades scored from two (1811-1820) to seventeen (1961-1970).

3. Linguistic diversity. The linguistic complexity of each country at the national level was classified according to the categories suggested by Criper and Ladefoged (1971). The language situation of a country was classified as *dominant* if the language spoken by its largest mother-tongue group was spoken natively by at least twice as many people as in the next largest mother-tongue group and if no other language was spoken natively by more than 10 percent of the population. The language situation of a country was classified as *predominant* if the language spoken by the largest mother-tongue group was spoken natively by twice as many people as were in the next largest mother-tongue group but there was also at least one language, in addition to the predominant one, that was spoken natively by at least 10 percent of the population. The language situation of a country was characterized as *mixed* if it was not classified as either dominant or predominant. These classifications were treated as three dichotomous variables, with each country being classified as belonging to only one. In addition, each country was classified with respect to the proportion of the population made up of the largest mother-tongue group and with respect to the communicability of the language spoken by the largest mother-tongue group. The latter variable was scored on a four-point scale, with the lowest point representing a language which was spoken in parts of the country only and the highest point representing a language spoken in more than three other countries.

4. Material benefits. No relatively direct index of the material benefits to be gained from learning English was employed, although it might have been possible, if expensive, to do so. Thus, for example, the proportion of help-wanted ads in the daily press which specified English as a requirement for employment might have been used. The measures used were the relative importance of English-speaking countries as suppliers of a country's imports and the relative importance of English-speaking countries as customers for a country's exports. Relative importance was scored in each case on a nine-point scale. While it is true that one need not know English in order to participate in foreign trade with English-speaking countries and while it is also true that direct participation in such trade represents a small proportion of a nation's gross national product, foreign trade may have a multiplier effect with respect to the material advantages associated with a knowledge of English. Thus, not only some of the employees of import-export firms might be expected to know the language of their principal customers but also some of the employees of the companies through which the imported or exported goods travel (manufac-

turers, wholesalers, retailers).

　　5.　Urbanization.　Urbanization was measured as the percentage of the population living in urban centers, as reported in the *World Data Handbook* of the United States Government (1972).

　　6.　Economic development.　The following measures were selected to represent economic development:　per capita gross national product, life expectancy, average daily caloric intake, and number of infant deaths per 1,000 live births. These statistics were taken from the *World Data Handbook* (U.S. Government, 1972).

　　7.　Educational development.　Four measures were employed to represent educational development.　These were the number of years of compulsory education, the proportion of the school-age population attending school, the proportion of the secondary school-age population enrolled in secondary school, and the rate of illiteracy.

　　8.　Religious composition.　The percentage of the population falling within each of the following categories was scored:　Roman Catholic, non-Roman Catholic Christian, Muslim, Hindu, Buddhist and Confucian, traditional beliefs, and other.

　　9.　Political affiliation.　Each nation was scored as belonging to one of four rather primitive categories:　neutral, leaning to the West, leaning toward the Soviet Union, or leaning toward China.　In addition, nations falling into either of the last two categories were also scored as belonging to a fifth category, leaning toward the East.

　　10.　Other variables.　In addition to the 30 predictor variables enumerated previously, the following 23 variables were employed:　population size, annual population increase, population density per square mile, total area, number of acres in the country per capita, percentage of total area used for agriculture, percentage of the labor force engaged in agriculture, gross national product, growth rate of the gross national product, growth rate of per capita income, number of radio receivers per 1,000 population, number of daily newspapers, television broadcasting, number of universities, public expenditure on education as a percentage of total public expenditure, total imports, total exports, proportion of imports from the United States, proportion of exports sent to the United States, English the official language of a neighboring country, extent of genetic relationship between English and the language spoken by the largest mother-tongue group, former Francophone colony, and former colony of a nation other than an Anglophone or Francophone country.

　　All in all, then, about 50 predictor (independent) variables were employed to predict each of six criterion (dependent) variables expressing the status of English around the world.

RESULTS

Before summarizing the intercorrelations and regression
analyses, we present some summary data with respect to the
status of English in the 102 countries surveyed.

English was the only official language or co-official language in 20 countries. In an additional 36 countries it held
a privileged status, i.e., it was used as a medium in courts,
as a principal medium of instruction in schools, or as the
chief foreign language employed by the government in its dealings with foreigners and with foreign governments. In only 38
countries did English have no official use whatsoever. In 56
countries it was the foreign language which most students were
taught first. Of the 88 countries for which data were available from Gage and Ohannessian (1974), English was a medium of
instruction throughout the secondary schools in 18 countries
and a subject of instruction throughout the secondary schools
in 61. It was a medium of instruction in at least some elementary schools in 15 of 88 countries and a subject of instruction in at least some elementary schools in 35 countries.
Gage and Ohannessian estimated that approximately 115 million
persons in the non-English mother-tongue states they surveyed
were exposed to English in the primary and secondary schools,
either as a medium or as a subject of instruction. Their data
with respect to the number of persons in English classes were
available for 87 of our countries. Of these, the average percentage of persons exposed to English in the schools was 6.3
percent.

When the status of English was examined according to
whether or not a country was a former Anglophone colony, there
were of course substantial differences. Thus, for example,
whereas almost 60 percent of the 29 former Anglophone colonies
for which we had information used English as a medium of instruction in at least some secondary schools, only 3 percent
of the other countries did so. Whereas all the former Anglophone colonies taught English as a subject in at least some
high schools, about two-thirds of the other countries did so.
Whereas almost 50 percent of the former Anglophone countries
used English as a medium of instruction in at least some primary schools, less than 2 percent of the other countries did
so. Finally, whereas almost three-fourths of the former Anglophone countries taught English as a subject of instruction in
at least some primary schools, less than one-fourth of the
other countries did so. With respect to the percentage of the
population exposed to English as a subject or medium of instruction in the primary and secondary schools, the average
percentage in the former Anglophone colonies was 11 percent as

contrasted with 4 percent in the average country which had never been an Anglophone colony. The sharpest difference between former Anglophone colonies and other countries with respect to the status of English can be found in terms of that language's official status. All the countries that employed English as their only official language or as a co-official language were former Anglophone colonies.

ZERO-ORDER CORRELATIONS

How well did the variables previously suggested — military imposition, duration of military rule, linguistic diversity, material benefits, urbanization, economic development, educational development, religious composition, and political affiliation — predict the status of English? Because there was a sharp difference between the former Anglophone colonies ($N=31$) and the other countries ($N=71$), it is worthwhile to examine these relationships not only for all countries combined but also separately for those countries that were never Anglophone colonies.

MILITARY IMPOSITION

We have already seen that there were substantial differences between former Anglophone colonies and other countries with respect to our six English criterion variables when expressed in terms of percentages. When expressed in terms of correlation coefficients, we see that former Anglophone colonial status was the single best predictor of five of these criteria, with coefficients ranging from .41 (use of English as a subject of instruction in secondary schools) to .77 (the composite criterion), with the median at .53. Former Anglophone colonial status was the third best predictor of the remaining criterion (use of English as a medium of instruction in primary schools), with a coefficient of .53. These coefficients are presented in Table 3.

DURATION OF COLONIAL RULE

There is a positive relationship between recency of independence and all but one of the criterion variables, but these relationships were modest ones. Excepting the use of English as a subject of instruction in secondary schools, which had a negligible relationship to recency of independence, the other criteria displayed correlation coefficients ranging from .25 (percent of the population in English classes) to .38 (use of English as a subject of instruction in primary schools). However, these relationships were largely due to the fact that almost half (31 of 64) of the former colonies had been former

TABLE 3

Relationship between Former Anglophone Colonial
Status and English Criterion Variables

Criterion	Correlation
Medium in secondary schools	.62
Medium in primary schools	.53
Subject in secondary schools	.41
Subject in primary schools	.53
Percentage of population in English classes	.50
Composite	.77

Anglophone dependencies. Most recently independent nations,
in other words, tended to be former Anglophone colonies, and
thus more recently independent nations tended to rely on English more than did countries that had been longer established.
When the correlations were computed only for those countries
which had never been Anglophone colonies, the positive relationship between recency of independence and the use of English in educational contexts disappeared. With respect to the
composite English criterion, a slight negative relationship
(minus .27) was found. Thus when former Anglophone colonies
were not considered, the more recently independent nations
tended to use English less, when measured in terms of the overall composite criterion. This negative relationship can be explained partly on the grounds that former Francophone colonies
(N=25), which presumably rely more heavily on French than on
English, tended to be more recently independent (r=.38). Thus
recency of statehood does not appear to have been independently related to the English criterion variables. The relationships between recency of independence and the criterion variables can be found in Table 4.

LINGUISTIC DIVERSITY

Former Anglophone colonies were found to be more linguistically diverse than the other countries. Whereas almost 80
percent of the countries which had never been Anglophone colonies were characterized as having a dominant language, only a
little over one-third of the former Anglophone colonies were

TABLE 4

Correlations between Recency of Independence and English
Criterion Variables

Criterion	All countries	All countries former Anglophone colonies
Medium in secondary schools	.35	-.04
Medium in primary schools	.35	.14
Subject in secondary schools	.06	-.21
Subject in primary schools	.38	.13
Percentage of population in English classes	.25	-.12
Composite	.27	-.27

so characterized. Conversely, whereas less than 10 percent of
the countries which had never been Anglophone colonies were described as linguistically mixed, about one-third of the former
Anglophone colonies were so described.

When coefficients were computed for all countries combined, linguistic diversity (language situation mixed) proved
to be positively correlated to all the English criterion variables. Substantial correlations were observed between linguistic diversity and use of English as a medium of instruction in
primary schools ($r=.64$) and secondary schools ($r=.58$). Even
after former Anglophone colonies had been excluded from consideration, substantial relationahips were observed between
linguistic diversity and these two criteria. Linguistic diversity was, in fact, the variable with the highest correlation with the use of English as a medium of instruction in primary school not only when the correlation was computed for all
countries combined ($r=.64$) but also when it was computed for
only those countries which had never been Anglophone colonies
($r=.70$). Thus linguistic diversity appeared to be related to
the use of English as a medium in the schools, particularly
primary schools, independently of former Anglophone colonial
status.

Three variables expressed linguistic homogeneity, relative
size of the largest mother-tongue group, communicability of the
language spoken by the largest mother-tongue group, and dominant language situation. These measures were inversely related
to the variable "mixed language situation," with correlation

coefficients in the .50s. The relationships between the homogeneity measures and the criterion variables were similar to
those between mixed language situation and the criterion measures except that, of course, the direction of the relationships
was reversed. The relationships between the linguistic diversity and the homogeneity measures on the one hand and the criterion variables on the other are presented in Table 5.

MATERIAL BENEFITS

. There was a modest positive relationship between the overall composite criterion and the relative importance of English-
speaking countries as customers for exports ($r=.38$). This coefficient was only slightly reduced ($r=.31$) when former Anglophone colonies were excluded, and in fact the relationship between former Anglophone colonial status and the relative importance of English-speaking countries to a nation's exports
was almost negligible ($r=.12$). Thus countries for which English-speaking nations were relatively important customers tended to have a greater overall use of English than countries for
which English-speaking nations were relatively less important,
and this relationship was independent of former Anglophone colonial status. The relationships between the export and import
variables with the criterion variables are shown in Table 6.

URBANISM, ECONOMIC DEVELOPMENT, AND EDUCATIONAL DEVELOPMENT

Urbanism, economic development, and educational development can be considered together as predictor variables because
they proved to be substantially correlated with one another
(see Table 7). Countries which were more urban also tended to
be more economically and educationally developed. The correlations between urbanism and the four measures of economic development ranged from .70 to .77; the correlations between urbanism and the four measures of educational development ranged
from .46 to .79, with three of these coefficients above .70;
and the correlations between the four measures of economic development and the four measures of educational development
ranged from .39 to .85, with the median coefficient at .77 and
with all but 4 of the 16 coefficients above .60. Only one of
these variables yielded substantially lower intercorrelations.
This was the number of years of compulsory education, whose
correlations with the other variables ranged from .39 to .51,
with the median coefficient at .45. The coefficients among
urbanism, economic development, and educational development,
which are presented in Table 7 for all countries combined, were
substantially the same when the former Anglophone colonies were
excluded.
    Urbanism, economic development, and educational develop-

TABLE 5

Correlations between Linguistic Diversity Measures and English Criterion Variables

Linguistic diversity measure	Countries	Medium in secondary schools	Medium in primary schools	Subject in secondary schools	Subject in primary schools	Percentage in English classes	Composite
Language situation — mixed	All	.58	.64	.24	.49	.23	.36
	Without former A-p colonies	.48	.70	.17	.23	-.13	.12
Language situation — predominant	All	.07	.09	.08	.03	.01	.14
	Without former A-p colonies	.20	-.05	-.03	-.04	-.05	.03
Language situation — dominant	All	-.46	-.51	-.23	-.36	-.17	-.36
	Without former A-p colonies	-.41	-.29	-.05	-.07	.11	-.06
Relative size of largest mother-tongue group	All	-.48	-.51	-.28	-.46	-.25	-.33
	Without former A-p colonies	-.26	-.29	-.22	-.26	-.10	-.10
Communicability of main language	All	-.50	-.51	-.11	-.51	-.25	-.42
	Without former A-p colonies	-.23	-.23	.03	-.34	-.04	-.14

TABLE 6

Correlations between the Relative Importance of Trade with English-Speaking Countries and the English Criterion Variables

Trade measure	Countries	Medium in secondary schools	Medium in primary schools	Subject in secondary schools	Subject in primary schools	Percentage in English classes	Composite
Exports	All	.30	.24	.20	.14	.11	.38
	Without former A-p colonies	.09	.01	.18	-.13	.00	.31
Imports	All	.09	.08	.27	-.04	.03	.22
	Without former A-p colonies	-.03	.05	.29	-.22	.05	.24

TABLE 7

Intercorrelations among Urbanism, Economic Development, and Educational Development Variables (All Countries)

Variable	1	2	3	4	5	6	7	8	9
1. Illiteracy	—	-.43	-.80	-.81	-.72	.84	-.76	-.85	-.71
2. Number of years of compulsory education		—	.51	.51	.46	-.46	.39	.43	.44
3. School enrollment ratio			—	.84	.76	-.78	.67	.78	.62
4. Secondary school enrollment ratio				—	.79	-.83	.78	.83	.84
5. Urbanism					—	-.77	.70	.76	.70
6. Infant death rate						—	-.67	-.85	-.72
7. Average daily calories							—	.76	.75
8. Life expectancy								—	.73
9. GNP (gross national product) per capita									—

ment were all modestly related to former Anglophone colonial status, which was negatively correlated to urbanism ($r=-.26$), number of years of compulsory education ($r=-.44$), school enrollment ratio ($r=-.26$), secondary school enrollment ratio ($r=-.27$), average caloric daily intake ($r=-.26$), and gross national product per capita ($r=-.25$), and which was positively related to the rate of illiteracy ($r=.28$). Former Anglophone colonies, in other words, showed a modest tendency to be less urbanized and less developed economically and educationally than other countries.

All the criterion variables except the proportion of the population enrolled in English classes showed modest relationships with most of these predictors when the correlations were computed for all countries combined. Countries which were less urbanized and less economically and educationally developed tended to place more reliance on English than did other countries. Because former Anglophone colonial status was related to these predictors, however, we can expect that some of these relationships disappeared when former Anglophone colonies were excluded. This in fact occurred for most criteria except the use of English as a medium of instruction in secondary schools and the use of English as a subject of instruction in secondary schools. The former criterion continued to display negative, although reduced, correlations with urbanism and with economic and educational development, and the latter criterion continued to show a negative, although reduced, relationship to economic development. The proportion of the population enrolled in primary and secondary school English classes, which showed negligible relationships with urbanism and with economic and educational development, when the correlations were computed for all countries combined, showed modest positive relationships with urbanism and with economic and educational development when the former Anglophone colonies were excluded. Thus, when former Anglophone colonies were removed from consideration, urbanism and economic and educational development were negatively related to the use of English as a medium of instruction in secondary schools and positively related to the proportion of the population enrolled in primary and secondary school English classes.

Developing nations apparently find it more difficult than other nations to provide secondary school education via indigenous languages. Expatriate teachers using foreign languages as media of instruction must sometimes be employed until the educational system can be sufficiently expanded to provide a sizable number of teachers who can teach via indigenous languages. Since it is usually more expensive to produce secondary school teachers than it is to produce primary school teachers, the widespread use of foreign languages as media of instruction is more commonly found at the secondary school level than at the primary school level. Thus there is a tendency for the widespread use of foreign languages as media of instruction in secondary schools to be more commonly found in poorer nations than in richer ones, which have greater resources for the development of teachers and materials and which can more readily afford to develop local languages for educational purposes.

The percentage of the population enrolled in primary and secondary school English classes, on the other hand, is partly a function of the proportion of the population enrolled in school, which in turn is a function of economic development. In general, the more economically developed a country, the greater the proportion of its population enrolled in school and therefore the greater the proportion of the population enrolled in English classes. The relationship between economic development and the proportion of the population enrolled in English classes was negligible when computed for all countries combined because former Anglophone colonies, which are typically poorer, also typically have a greater proportion of the population enrolled in English classes. The relationship could be seen when these countries were excluded from the computation. The correlations of urbanism, economic development, and

educational development with the criterion variables can be
seen in Table 8.

RELIGIOUS COMPOSITION

The only religious category to be substantially correlated with the criterion variables was that of "traditional beliefs," i.e., local systems of folk beliefs as distinguished
from universal religions or religions associated with high cultures such as those of Christianity, Hinduism, and Islam.   The
highest of these correlations were with the use of English as
a medium of instruction in primary schools ($r=.62$) and in secondary schools ($r=.53$).   The substantial relationships with
these two variables remained when former Anglophone colonies
were excluded from the computations.   (The correlation between
former Anglophone colonial status and the traditional belief
percentage was only .21.)   These relationships can be explained in part by the fact that countries with relatively high pro-
portions of the population categorized as subscribing to traditional beliefs tended to be relatively unurbanized and relatively undeveloped economically and educationally.   The correlation between the traditional belief percentage, on the one
hand, and urbanism and the economic and educational development indices, on the other, ranged from .28 to .55, when computed for all countries combined, with five of these nine coefficients above .40.   Countries with high traditional belief
percentages, furthermore, tended to be linguistically mixed
($r=.50$).   While linguistic diversity itself was negatively related to urbanism and to economic and educational development,
these relationships were on the whole smaller than between the
traditional belief percentage and the urbanism, economic development, and educational development indices.   The relationships
between linguistic diversity and the urbanism and development
indices ranged from .12 to .46, with only two of the nine coefficients above .40.   These relationships were about the same
when computed without the former Anglophone colonies.   Thus
the localism reflected both by traditional beliefs and by linguistic diversity were substantially related to reliance upon
English as a medium of instruction in the schools, this reliance being mediated at least in part by lack of economic development.   The correlations between the traditional beliefs percentage and the criterion variables are presented in Table 9,
and the relationships of linguistic diversity to the traditional belief percentage, urbanism, and the economic and educational development indices are presented in Table 10.

TABLE 8

Correlations of Urbanism, Economic Development, and Educational Development Variables with English Criterion Variables

Variable	Countries	Medium in secondary schools	Medium in primary schools	Subject in secondary schools	Subject in primary schools	Percentage in English classes	Composite
Percent of population urban	All	-.42	-.41	-.16	-.36	-.02	-.26
	Without former A-p colonies	-.30	-.19	-.03	-.02	.33	.07
Infant death rate	All	.45	.39	.37	.28	.01	.19
	Without former A-p colonies	.26	.12	.32	-.24	-.57	-.13
Daily caloric intake	All	-.33	-.27	-.31	-.18	-.04	-.27
	Without former A-p colonies	-.24	-.18	-.23	.09	.27	-.11
Life expectancy	All	-.33	-.32	-.32	-.18	.08	-.16
	Without former A-p colonies	-.23	-.12	-.26	.14	.53	.00

GNP per capita	All	-.33	-.28	-.33	-.11	.06	-.21
	Without former A-p colonies	-.17	-.12	-.26	.30	.47	.10
Illiteracy	All	.33	.29	.24	.16	-.04	.16
	Without former A-p colonies	.23	.07	.13	-.20	-.41	-.18
Number of years of compulsory education	All	-.54	-.42	-.24	-.26	-.13	-.46
	Without former A-p colonies	-.25	.05	-.09	.40	.45	.02
School enrollment ratio	All	-.34	-.32	-.21	-.23	.14	-.21
	Without former A-p colonies	-.23	-.02	-.11	.06	.39	.03
Secondary school enrollment ratio	All	-.43	-.38	-.29	-.28	.04	-.27
	Without former A-p colonies	-.24	-.15	-.18	.09	.45	.06

TABLE 9

Correlations between the Traditional Beliefs Percentage and the English Criterion Variables

Criterion	All countries	All countries but former Anglophone colonies
Medium in secondary schools	.53	.56
Medium in primary schools	.62	.65
Subject in secondary schools	.23	.17
Subject in primary schools	.49	.24
Percentage of population in English classes	.21	-.15
Composite	.22	-.15

POLITICAL AFFILIATION

Political affiliation, in terms of associations with the Big Powers, proved to have little relationship to the criterion variables. None of the five political categories had a substantial correlation with any of the criterion variables. The highest coefficient observed, when computed for all countries, was .19. When computed without the former Anglophone colonies, the highest coefficient was .22.

THE HIGHEST ZERO-ORDER CORRELATIONS BETWEEN PREDICTORS AND CRITERIA

When correlations were computed across all countries, the single most important predictor of the criterion variables was former Anglophone colonial status. With coefficients ranging from .41 (use of English as a subject of instruction in secondary schools) to .77 (the overall composite), it proved to be the best single predictor for five of the six criteria. The second best predictor was linguistic diversity (mixed language situation), which was the single best predictor of the use of English as a medium of instruction in primary schools (r=.64) and which was the second best predictor of the use of English as a medium of instruction in secondary schools (r=.58). (A related measure, the communicability of the language spoken by the largest mother-tongue group, was the second best predictor

TABLE 10

*Correlations between Linguistic Diversity (Language Situation —
Mixed) and Selected Variables*

Variable	All countries	All countries but former Anglophone colonies
Traditional beliefs percent	.50	.73
Percent population urban	-.38	-.40
Infant death rate	.44	.46
Daily caloric intake	-.31	-.24
Life expectancy	-.46	-.49
GNP per capita	-.28	-.22
Illiteracy	.38	.37
Number of years compulsory education	-.12	-.18
School enrollment ratio	-.36	-.37
Secondary school enrollment ratio	-.36	-.33

of the use of English as a subject of instruction in primary
schools ($r=-.51$).) The third best predictor of the criteria
was the percentage of the population whose religion was categorized as that of traditional beliefs. This was the second
and third best predictor of the use of English in primary
schools, as a medium ($r=.62$) and as a subject ($r=.49$) of instruction. Another good predictor was the number of years of
compulsory education, which was the second highest predictor
of the overall composite ($r=-.46$) and which was the third best
predictor of the use of English as a medium of instruction in
secondary schools ($r=-.54$).

When the former Anglophone colonies were excluded from
the computations, the single best predictors of the criteria
were linguistic diversity and the traditional beliefs percentage. These were either the best or second best predictors for
the use of English as a medium of instruction in secondary and
primary schools, with the four coefficients ranging from .48
to .70. Number of years of compulsory education was the best
predictor of the use of English as a subject of instruction in

primary school (*r*=.40). The best single predictors of the proportion of the population studying in primary and secondary school English classes were the infant mortality rate (*r*=-.57) and life expectancy (*r*=.53). The best single predictor of the overall composite criterion was percentage of exports of English-speaking countries (*r*=.31).

All in all, then, when former Anglophone colonial status was not considered, the best predictors of the criteria were linguistic diversity, traditional beliefs percentage, number of years of compulsory education, economic development indicators, and exports to English-speaking countries. In general, countries with greater linguistic diversity, a greater traditional beliefs percentage, fewer years of compulsory education, and relatively less economic development tended to place greater reliance on English both as a medium of instruction and as a subject of instruction. Conversely, countries which were more economically developed tended to have a greater percentage of the population enrolled in primary and secondary school English classes.

As we have seen, the interrelationships among these predictors were complex. How much did each contribute to the prediction of the criteria when the predictors were combined with one another? To answer this question we turn to the multiple regression analyses.

MULTIPLE REGRESSION ANALYSES

Just as a zero-order correlation coefficient expresses the degree of relationship between two variables, a multiple correlation coefficient expresses the degree of relationship between a criterion variable and two or more predictor variables taken together. In general, multiple correlation coefficient will be higher than a zero-order correlation coefficient to the extent that the multiple correlation combines predictors which have high correlations with the criterion and low correlations with one another.

Just as a zero-order coefficient squared expresses the percentage of the variation (variance) of one variable that is associated with or "accounted for" by the other, so the multiple correlation coefficient squared expresses the percentage of the criterion's variance that is associated with or accounted for by the predictor variables jointly. Multiple regression analysis tells us how much additional variation in the criterion variable is associated with the addition of a new predictor.

Let us take as a concrete example the use of English as a medium of instruction in secondary schools. The single best predictor of this criterion was former Anglophone colonial status (r=.62). Another variable with a high correlation with this criterion was the traditional beliefs percentage (r=.53). Adding traditional beliefs percentage to former Anglophone colonial status increased the percentage of the criterion's variance that we can account for only to the extent that these two predictor variables did not overlap with one another. In fact they were related to one another slightly (r=.21). Thus, adding traditional beliefs percentage to former Anglophone colonial status increased the correlation of .62 (between the criterion and former Anglophone colonial status only) to .75. If we square each of these coefficients and then subtract the smaller from the larger figure we find a difference of 17 percent. In other words, by adding traditional beliefs percentage to former Anglophone colonial status we can account for an additional 17 percent of the variance in the use of English as a medium of instruction in secondary school.

We present the following results from our multiple regression analyses for each of the criterion variables in turn, based on all countries. For each regression analysis we show the effects of including each additional predictor variable until the addition of a predictor results in an increment of *less* than 4 percent in the amount of the criterion's variance that has been "accounted for" or "explained." Each additional predictor resulting in an increment of at least 4 percent, in other words, is shown. In the tables summarizing these results, the following symbols are used:

R = multiple correlation coefficient

R^2 = square of the multiple correlation coefficient
This expresses the proportion of the criterion's variance which has been "explained" by the predictor variables up to and including the new predictor.

ΔR^2 = increment in R^2. This is the increment in the proportion of the criterion's variance that has been explained" by adding the new predictor.

r = the zero-order correlation coefficient between the additional predictor variable and the criterion variable.

THE USE OF ENGLISH AS A MEDIUM OF INSTRUCTION IN SECONDARY SCHOOLS

By combining the traditional beliefs percentage, exports to English-speaking countries, and linguistic diversity (mixed language situation) to former Anglophone colonial status as a predictor of the use of English as medium of instruction in secondary schools, we obtained a multiple correlation of almost .82. These results are presented in Table 11.

TABLE 11

Multiple Regression Analysis: Use of English as a Medium of Instruction in Secondary Schools[a]

Step	Variable	R	R^2	ΔR^2	r
1	Former Anglophone colony	.623	.388	.388	.623
2	Traditional beliefs percent	.747	.558	.170	.535
3	Exports to English-speaking countries	.790	.624	.066	.302
4	Language situation — mixed	.819	.671	.046	.583

[a] All steps shown until first step at which ΔR^2 fell below .036.

THE USE OF ENGLISH AS A MEDIUM OF INSTRUCTION IN PRIMARY SCHOOLS

The single best predictor of the use of English as a medium of instruction in primary schools was linguistic diversity ($r=.64$). By adding the traditional beliefs percentage, former Anglophone colonial status, exports to English-speaking countries, and percentage Hindu, the multiple correlation coefficient rose to .84 (see Table 12). It should be noted that the last of these predictors was negligibly correlated with the criterion but nevertheless raised the proportion of variance accounted for by 4 percent. A predictor which is not correlated to a criterion can sometimes raise the multiple correlation coefficient by serving as a "suppression variable," if it correlates substantially with another predictor variable which is correlated with the criterion. In the present case, percentage Hindu was correlated with former Anglophone colonial status ($r=.36$), which in turn was correlated with the criterion. Former Anglophone colonial status contained some variance which was not shared with the criterion and which reduced the correlation that otherwise might have been obtained with the criterion. Presumably some of this "unwanted" or useless variance that was unshared with the criterion was shared with percentage Hindu, which acted in such a way as to "suppress" the effect of part of the unwanted variance, thus raising the contribution that could be made by former Anglophone colonial status to the prediction of the criterion.

TABLE 12

Multiple Regression Analysis: Use of English as a Medium of Instruction in Primary Schools[a]

Step	Variable	R	R^2	ΔR^2	r
1	Language situation — mixed	.639	.408	.408	.639
2	Traditional beliefs percent	.729	.531	.123	.624
3	Former Anglophone colony	.797	.635	.103	.530
4	Exports to English-speaking countries	.819	.671	.036	.244
5	Percentage Hindu	.844	.712	.040	-.013

[a] All steps shown until first step at which ΔR^2 fell below .036.

Three variables, then, in addition to former Anglophone colonial status, were important in the multiple prediction of the use of English as a medium of instruction both in primary schools and in secondary schools: linguistic diversity, the traditional beliefs percentage, and exports to English-speaking countries.

THE USE OF ENGLISH AS A SUBJECT OF INSTRUCTION IN PRIMARY SCHOOLS

Three variables increased our ability to account for variance in the use of English as a subject of instruction in primary schools by more than 3 percent when added to former Anglophone colonial status (see Table 13). These were, in order, the traditional beliefs percentage, the non-Roman Catholic Christian percentage, and the relative size of the largest mother-tongue community. The last of these was in part an inverse measure of linguistic diversity (r=.52). Thus religious composition and linguistic diversity appeared to be important predictors for this criterion, much as they were for the use of English as a medium of instruction in secondary and primary schools.

TABLE 13

Multiple Regression Analysis: Use of English as a Subject of Instruction in Primary Schools[a]

Step	Variable	R	R^2	ΔR^2	r
1	Former Anglophone colony	.533	.284	.284	.533
2	Traditional beliefs percent	.659	.435	.151	.493
3	Percent non-Roman Catholic Christian	.717	.514	.079	.114
4	Relative size of largest mother-tongue community	.754	.568	.054	-.460

[a] All steps shown until first step at which ΔR^2 fell below .036.

ENGLISH AS A SUBJECT OF INSTRUCTION IN SECONDARY SCHOOLS

Six variables in addition to former Anglophone colonial status added at least 4 percent to the incremental prediction of English as a subject of instruction in secondary schools (see Table 14), yielding a multiple correlation coefficient of .75. These were, in order, status as a former colony of a non-Anglophone, non-Francophone power, infant death rate, percentage of the population living in urban areas, percentage Buddhist and Confucianists, percentage of illiteracy, and number of acres per capita (total area of the country divided by the population). All but the last of these, for the incremental contribution of which we can advance no principled explanation, was a measure either of urbanism, religious composition, former colonial rule, or economic development. The multiple prediction of this criterion, then, contrasts with that of the three criteria previously described — the use of English as a medium of instruction in secondary and in primary schools and the use of English as a subject of instruction in primary schools — which did not include urbanism, economic development, or educational development among their important incremental predictors. It may be recalled that these three criteria were substantially related to one another but only moderately related to the use of English as a subject of instruction in secondary schools. It is of interest that the addition of urbanism and illiteracy improved prediction although an economic development variable, to which both were substantially related, had entered the multiple correlation before them. Thus economic development, urbanism, and educational development were in part independently related to the use of English as a subject of instruction in secondary schools.

TABLE 14

Multiple Regression Analysis: Use of English as a Subject of Instruction in Secondary Schools[a]

Step	Variable	R	R^2	ΔR^2	r
1	Former Anglophone colony	.415	.172	.172	.415
2	Former non-Anglophone, non-Francophone colony	.512	.262	.090	-.374
3	Infant death rate	.575	.330	.068	.369
4	Percent of population urban	.632	.399	.069	-.159
5	Percentage Buddhists	.683	.466	.067	.104
6	Illiteracy	.717	.514	.048	.241
7	Acres per capita	.750	.562	.048	-.200

[a] All steps shown until first step at which ΔR^2 fell below .036.

PERCENTAGE OF THE POPULATION STUDYING ENGLISH IN PRIMARY AND SECONDARY SCHOOLS

Four variables improved prediction by as much as 4 percent when added to former Anglophone colonial status as predictors of the proportion of the population studying English in primary and secondary schools (see Table 15). These were, in order, proportion of the school-age population enrolled in school, relative size of the largest mother-tongue community, genetic relationship to English of the language spoken by the largest mother-tongue community, and Western political affiliation. The importance of the next-to-last of these is probably due to the fact that non-Indo-European languages tend to be spoken in countries which are less economically and educationally developed, less urbanized, and less homogeneous linguistically. (India, of course, is a notable exception to this tendency.) Although the school-enrollment ratio had a low correlation

TABLE 15

Multiple Regression Analysis: The Percentage of the Population Enrolled in Primary and Secondary School English Classes[a]

Step	Variable	R	R^2	ΔR^2	r
1	Former Anglophone colony	.499	.249	.249	.499
2	School enrollment ratio	.570	.325	.076	.138
3	Relative size of largest mother-tongue community	.653	.427	.101	-.251
4	Genetic relationship to English of main language	.695	.483	.056	-.310
5	Political affiliation — Western	.721	.520	.037	.195

[a] All steps shown until first step at which ΔR^2 fell below .036.

with the criterion ($r=.14$), it had a moderate correlation with it after the non-Anglophone countries had been removed from consideration ($r=.39$). Important incremental contributions, then, were made to the prediction of the proportion of the population enrolled in English classes, by variables assessing both linguistic diversity (in this case, homogeneity) and educational development, which had not appeared together as important incremental predictors of the other criteria.

OVERALL COMPOSITE VARIABLE

The overall composite variable represented both educational and noneducational variables with respect to the status of English, including its status as a language of administration and its use in mass media (see Table 1). It was substantially predicted by former Anglophone colonial status ($r=.77$). Only two additional variables contributed incrementally more than 3 percent to the prediction of the criterion (see Table 16). These were, in order, exports to English-speaking countries and the communicability of the language spoken by the largest mother-tongue group. The second of these was in part an inverse measure of linguistic diversity ($r=-.53$). Relative importance of English-speaking countries to exports, which was an important incremental contributor to the use of English as a medium of instruction in secondary and in primary schools, was also an important contributor to the incremental prediction of the overall composite criterion. Similarly, linguistic diversity (or homogeneity), important in three of the other four criteria, was also important in the cumulative prediction of the composite criterion. Absent as important incremental contributors of this criterion, however, were variables indicating economic or educational development, which were important to the multiple prediction of the use of English as a subject of instruction in secondary schools and the proportion of the population enrolled in primary and secondary school English classes.

TABLE 16

Multiple Regression Analysis: Overall English Composite Criterion[a]

Step	Variable	R	R^2	ΔR^2	r
1	Former Anglophone colony	.766	.586	.586	.766
2	Exports to English-speaking countries	.819	.671	.084	.378
3	Communicability of language of largest mother-tongue group	.844	.712	.041	-.423

[a] All steps shown until first step at which ΔR^2 fell below .036.

SUMMARY OF THE MULTIPLE REGRESSION ANALYSES

Table 17 indicates the categories of variables which contributed at least a 4 percent increment to the multiple prediction of each of the criterion variables: former colonial status, linguistic diversity, material benefits, urbanization, economic development, educational development, religious composition, and political affiliation. It can be seen that the most important contributors, in addition to former colonial status, were religious composition and linguistic diversity, each contributing incrementally to four or five of the six criteria. The next most important was the relative importance of English-speaking countries to exports, contributing to the incremental prediction of three criteria. Educational development variables contributed to two, and variables indicating

TABLE 17

Categories of Variables Contributing at Least 4 Percent to the Incremental Prediction of the English Criteria

Category	Percentage added[a]					
	Medium in secondary schools	Medium in primary schools	Subject in secondary schools	Subject in primary schools	Percentage in English classes	Composite
Former colonial status	39	10	26[b]	28	25	59
Linguistic diversity/homogeneity	05	41	—	05	10	04
Economic incentives (exports)	07	04	—	—	—	08
Urbanism	—	—	07	—	—	—
Economic development	—	—	07	—	—	—
Educational development	—	—	05	—	08	—
Religious composition	17	16[b]	07	23[b]	—	—
Political affiliation	—	—	—	—	04	—
Other	—	—	05	—	06	—

[a] Percentage contribution to the multiple prediction of criterion variance until the first step at which ΔR^2 fell below .036.

[b] Sum of the incremental contribution of two predictors.

urbanism, economic development, and political affiliation each
contributed to the multiple prediction of one criterion.

SUMMARY AND CONCLUSIONS

    Statistics were gathered from secondary sources for 102
non-English-mother-tongue countries with respect both to the
status of English and to economic, educational, demographic,
and other variables in an attempt to determine which variables,
singly and in combination, are related to the use of English
as an additional language around the world. We hypothesized
that the variables isolated by Brosnahan (1963) with respect
to the spread of Arabic, Greek, and Latin as mother tongues —
military imposition, duration of authority, linguistic diversity, and material advantages — would also be related to the
spread of English as an additional language. We also hypothesized that five additional factors would be related to this
expansion — urbanization, economic development, educational development, religious composition, and political affiliation.
Of these nine categories, we found that all but political affiliation showed at least a moderate relationship to the status
of English. However, the direction of the relationships depended on the criterion. Urbanization and economic and educational development were positively related to the percentage
of the population enrolled in primary and secondary school English classes when former Anglophone colonies were excluded from
consideration, but negatively correlated to the other criterion variables. Poorer countries, in other words, were more
likely to rely on English as a medium of instruction and to
stress English as a subject of instruction than were richer nations, but poorer nations were less likely to provide equal opportunity to learn English through formal schooling.
    The most important categories of predictor, in terms of
their zero-order correlations with the English criteria, were
former Anglophone colonial status, linguistic diversity, religious composition, and educational and economic development.
The most important categories in terms of their incremental
contribution to the prediction of the status of English, after
former Anglophone colonial status had been considered, were religious composition and linguistic diversity followed by material benefits (exports to English-speaking countries). Urbanism and economic and educational development indicators contributed relatively little, independently of the other predictors.
    It is of interest that exports to English-speaking coun-
tries proved to be a better predictor, both singly and jointly,
than imports. This result is reminiscent of the finding that
in Ethiopian markets, sellers accommodated themselves to buy-

ers by using the latters' language (Cooper and Carpenter, 1969).
That exports were a better predictor than imports provides additional support for the notion that material gains provide an
important incentive for second-language acquisition inasmuch
as it is plausible that all things being equal (which of course
is rarely the case) one has more incentive to learn the language of one's customers than of one's suppliers.

Seven of the nine categories of predictor variables were
related both singly and jointly to the spread of English as an
additional language. Political affiliation, which showed at
best a very slight relationship to the status of English, contributed incrementally to the prediction of one of the criteria. Conversely, duration of military rule, while moderately
related to the status of English, showed no independent relationship to the criterion variables, after former Anglophone
colonial status had been considered. It is likely that the
duration of military rule is more important for the spread of
a language as a mother tongue than as an additional language.

This study has taken numerals, found in the small print
of books, and related them to one another. It is sometimes
easy to forget that these numerals reflect, if palely and imperfectly and waveringly, human activities and human passions.
To say that English is spreading around the world as a function of the combination of particular variables is a summarizing statement, based on the effects of innumerable human interactions and motivations. Individuals, not countries, learn
English as an additional language. An individual learns English, moreover, not because of abstractions such as linguistic
diversity or international trade balances but because the knowledge of English helps him to communicate in contexts in which,
for economic or educational or emotional reasons, he wants to
communicate and because the opportunity to learn English is
available to him. That the summarizing statistics employed
here revealed pleasing symmetries and sensible regularities
should not allow us to forget the human behavior underlying
them. The study of language spread, then, must proceed not only from the manipulation and analysis of summary data at very
great levels of abstraction but also from the observation of
human behavior at first hand. Why do particular individuals
in particular contexts want to learn English? How do they go
about learning it? What are the circumstances in which they
use it once they have learned it? What effect does their knowledge of English have upon their knowledge and usage of other
languages? Primary data of great contextual specificity must
be sought, as well as secondary data far removed from the everyday arenas in which languages are learned and used and aban-
doned, if we are to construct a satisfactory explanation of
language maintenance and language shift in general and of the
expansion and decline of languages of wider communication in
particular.

REFERENCES

Alexandre, P.   A few observations on language use among Cam-
      eroonese *elite* families. In W.H. Whiteley (Ed.), *Language
      use and social change*. London: Oxford University Press,
      1971. Pp. 254-261.
Brosnahan, L.F.   Some historical cases of language imposition.
      In J. Spencer (Ed.), *Language in Africa*. Cambridge:
      Cambridge University Press, 1963, Pp. 7-24.
Cooper, R.L.   The spread of Amharic. In M.L. Bender et al.,
      Language in Ethiopia. London: Oxford University Press,
      1975. Pp. 289-301.
Cooper, R.L., and Carpenter, S.   Linguistic diversity in the
      Ethiopian market. *Journal of African Languages,* 1969, *8*
      (Part 3), 160-168.
Cooper, R.L., and Horvath, R.J.   Language, migration, and
      urbanization in Ethiopia. *Anthropological Linguistics,*
      1973, *15*, 221-243.
Criper, C., and Ladefoged, P.   Linguistic complexity in
      Uganda. In W.H. Whiteley (Ed.), *Language use and social
      change*. London: Oxford University Press, 1971. Pp. 145-
      159.
Gage, W.W., and Ohannessian, S.   ESOL enrollments throughout
      the world. *The Linguistic Reporter,* 1974, *16,* (9), 13-16.
Scotton, C.M.   *Choosing a lingua franca in an African capital*.
      Edmonton and Champaign: Linguistic Research, 1972.
U.S. Government, Department of State.   *World data handbook*.
      Washington, D.C.: U.S. Government Printing Office,
      1972. (Department of State Publication 8665, General
      Foreign Policy Series 264.)

Chapter 9

Some Observations Concerning
Bilingualism and Second-Language
Teaching in Developing Countries
and in North America

G. RICHARD TUCKER

McGill University

During the past eight years, I have had the opportunity
to observe closely and to begin to examine empirically diverse
aspects of the role of language in education in a variety of
sociocultural settings. Specifically, I have worked as a professor, researcher, and language-teaching advisor in Southeast
Asia (the Philippines), the Middle East and Africa (Egypt, Jordan, Lebanon, Algeria, Nigeria), Haiti, and, of course, in
Canada (Tucker & d'Anglejan, 1975).
I have been associated with a variety of institutions
where the goals were to devise comprehensive second-language
teaching programs with emphasis on both the theoretical and
the applied aspects of language learning and language teaching.
The Philippines, for example, represents a country with a bilingual educational system where neither of the two official
languages (Philipino — the national language, or English — the
language of wider communication) is spoken natively by a majority of the citizenry. In the Middle East there exist great
economic and social pressures for individuals to develop proficiency in a second language such as English where the majority of individuals speak natively a colloquial form of Arabic —
a language whose classical form differs from the colloquial
and, of course, from English. The differences between the or-
thographic system of Arabic and English pose additional difficulties for the student.
In Nigeria, educators are now experimenting with educational programs that will involve the use of the local vernacular language (e.g., Hausa, Igbo, Yoruba) as the major medium
of instruction throughout the six-year primary cycle with English taught as a second language one period per day. English,

however, remains the national language of the country and will continue to be used for secondary and post-secondary education.

In the Maghreb, the Algerians have decided to Arabize, Algerianize and democratize the educational system with the result that Arabic is rapidly replacing French (no longer an official language of the country) as a medium of instruction, and the demand for English is growing at an incredible rate. In Haiti, we are experimenting with a bidialectal educational program in which children are introduced to school instruction via Creole and subsequently bridged into standard French (de Ronceray, 1975).

In this chapter, I would like to identify several factors that seem to me to affect the choice or utilization of a language for instructional purposes in many developing countries. Then, I would like to comment on potential educational developments in these countries and contrast these developments with those in North America. In a recent report Melvin Fox (1975, p. 20) has noted:

> In the 1950s both host governments and their external supporters tended to view technical assistance as a simple unilateral transfer of knowledge and to assume that given the "right" education (in effect, the kind of education developed nations could supply in certain fields), appropriate changes would occur. Because the necessary knowledge was available principally in countries using world languages, it was assumed modernization could be made accessible to all who would learn those languages. These assumptions have been questioned as it has become clear that patterns of development in different countries are far more diverse and complex than was originally realized, and that therefore the use of local languages may be indispensable for the development of cultural identity and for the communication of necessary social, political, or educational innovations by local leaders.

Thus, in many countries, decisions have recently been made to decrease the use of a foreign language as a medium of instruction in that country's schools (e.g., the Philippines, the Sudan, Algeria) or even to decrease the amount of time devoted to teaching the foreign language as a subject (e.g., Jordan, the Sudan). These decisions seem to be associated with, among other things, the introduction of *universal primary education*, the desire to develop permanent *functional literacy* for the greatest possible number of citizens, a concern with the *surrender value* of education, and a belief that a sense of national or ethnic awareness and *national identity* can best be encouraged by the use of an indigenous language as the major medium of instruction at school rather than an ex-

ternally imposed language of wider communication. However, despite the decisions in some countries to decrease the time al-
lotted for foreign-language instruction, certain citizens of
these countries retain a demonstrated need for greater foreign-
language proficiency than ever before. One important implication of this apparent paradox is that contemporary programs of
foreign-language instruction must be much more efficient than
previous programs.

Given the complex set of social and political factors
which presently affect the role of language in education, it
is my belief that the program of bilingual education now being
implemented in the Philippines (Sibayan, in press); the program
of vernacularization with improved ESL (English as a second
language) training in Nigeria (Fafunwa, 1975); the program of
Arabization coupled with the development of a new series of
foreign-language institutes in Algeria; and others, now under
way in many countries, will result in radical transformations
within the affected societies — the relevant educational experiences to which a large number of citizens will now have
access should serve to increase human potential through enhancing the level of individual maturity and hence should increase
the range of human choices. As you can, no doubt infer, I am
very optimistic about recent educational innovations in many
of the so-called developing countries in which I have recently
worked.

I am much less sanguine, however, when I consider the contemporary North American setting. During the past ten years
or so, educators have been called upon to make some dramatic
changes in their policies and practices to take into account
the cultural diversity inherent in North American society.
One of the greatest challenges which we are now facing is that
of providing effective second-language teaching within the context of the public school system, while simultaneously nurturing the native-language development and sociocultural traditions of heterogeneous student populations. The challenge is
a very serious one. In some countries — the United States, for
instance — failure to achieve this goal could lead to the increased alienation of large immigrant and indigenous populations, and to acute social distress. In Canada, if we cannot
make bilingualism or at least an appreciation of bilingualism
a fact of life throughout the country, our present political
structure will not survive.

The need to provide effective second-language teaching to
such a large segment of our population poses a very serious
challenge for each and every one of us — and for me at least,
the implications of this challenge far transcend the question
(albeit an important one now being discussed by many educators,
applied linguists, etc.) of the validity of habit formation
versus creative construction as an explanatory concept. In

fact, I would like to suggest that theoretical validity or methodological sophistication may be relatively minor ingredients in the development of a successful and total second-language education program.

Let me digress for just a moment to share with you two vignettes that have affected me very much:

I am dismayed by the reports of research such as that conducted by Frank Jones and Wallace Lambert (1965) in Canada a number of years ago where they found that Canadians, in general, favored immigration, but that they believed there should be strict minimum educational and occupational criteria for admission (e.g., doctors, lawyers, would be welcome). Paradoxically the respondents reported that they would not even consider using the professional services of these newcomers — rather the newcomers should form the core of the agricultural and service force needed to develop the Canadian interior.

Second, I am continually dismayed at home in Canada — an officially bilingual country where the federal government is currently subsidizing second-language teaching to the extent of several hundreds of millions of dollars each year in schools and in the public sector — that there are some fully (demonstrably and admittedly) bilingual individuals who refuse to function (in their jobs as representatives of the federal government) in one of the country's two official languages.

These vignettes, and I am sure that there are thousands of others like them, disturb me because I wonder whether it matters at all if we better understand the *process* of second-language acquisition when one criterion for obtaining a job is mastery of standard American English; but where the Chicano or the Franco-American who speaks standard American English won't get the job anyway.

What I want to suggest today is that the attitudes of the community at large — the attitudes of "Middle America" — toward minority-group members are of crucial importance: it is here I believe that we must focus our attention.

How often have you noticed that when there exist favorable attitudes or tolerance on the part of the dominant group toward members of the other ethnic groups, TESL (teaching English as a second language) programs or bilingual education are almost unnecessary (e.g., consider the case of many central European Jews who migrated to Canada and of many Scandinavians)? And how often have you noticed that where there exist unfavorable attitudes on the part of the dominant group, TESL programs or bilingual education programs are never sufficient (e.g., with many Chicanos, Franco-Americans)?

The message that I want to convey is that I believe that TESL teachers and bilingual education teachers are well motivated and well trained and that they are preparing their students with the linguistic building blocks which are needed to function in an English-speaking society.

But I seriously question whether at this time society is prepared to receive their product. The central problem facing us as I see it is to reach the "dominant-group American" (the Middle American, if you will). Here, where most people have never heard of ESL, have never heard of TESL, have never heard of bilingual education, sensitivity to cultural diversity must be driven home. For this reason, I am excited when I am in the United States to learn about the Culver City project of Russell Campbell and Andrew Cohen and his colleagues at the University of California in Los Angeles (Cohen, 1974) where Anglo children in a Los Angeles suburb are participating in an intensive Spanish program together with Spanish-Americans. For this same reason, I was excited when Wallace Lambert spoke at the Denver TESOL (Teachers of English to Speakers of Other Languages) meeting in 1974 about the importance of "people studies" for monolingual-monocultural Americans. At this time when so many tens of millions of dollars are being spent on developing innovative programs for minority-group Americans, can we afford not to take every opportunity to maximize the chances that there will be a place for the minority-group child in North American society and that he will not be constrained by his ethnic, racial, or social origin?

When society is prepared to receive this product, when our educational system permits every child to increase the range of choices available to him, then — and only then — will second-language teaching or bilingual education programs (to paraphrase Eliane Condon) at last become associated with "quality" rather than "compensatory" education. Until such a time, North America — it seems to me — in contrast to the countries of the third world must be regarded very much as a developing country with regard to its educational system.

REFERENCES

Cohen, A.D.   The Culver City Spanish immersion program: The
     first two years. *The Modern Language Journal,* 1974, *58,*
     95-103.
Fafunwa, A.B.   The six-year primary project: Second phase.
     Mimeo. University of Ife, Ile-Ife, Nigeria, 1975.
Fox, M.J.   *Language in education: Problems and prospects*
     in research and training. New York: The Ford Foundation,
     1975.
Jones, F.E., & Lambert, W.E.   Occupational rank and attitudes
     toward immigrants. *Public Opinion Quarterly,* 1965, *29,*
     137-144.
de Ronceray, H.   Project experimental sur le bilinguisme

créole-français. *Bulletin d'Information du Chiss*, 1975, *14*, 4.

Sibayan, B.P.   Bilingual education in the Philippines. In B. Spolsky & R.L. Cooper (Eds.), *Case studies in bilingual education*. Rowley, Mass.: Newbury House, (in press).

Tucker, G.R., & d'Anglejan, A.   New directions in second language teaching. In R. Troike & N. Modiano (Eds.), *Proceedings of the first interamerican conference on bilingual education*. Arlington, Va.: Center for Applied Linguistics, 1975.   Pp. 63-72.

Chapter 10

Summary and Discussion

FRED GENESEE

The Protestant School Board of Greater Montreal

There has been a recent upsurge of interest in all things bilingual including a renewed and invigorated investigation of some traditional issues and a growing interest in new and diverse aspects of bilingualism. We have, I think, in the present proceedings a comprehensive sampling of these different areas of interest. The chapters in this volume can be fitted into three general themes which, I think, do minimum injustice to these reports and which reflect major issues in the entire field of bilingual research. They include: (1) the cognitive and social consequences of bilingualism for the individual (as represented by the chapters by Ben-Zeev, McCormack, and Lambert); (2) bilingual communities (as represented by the contributions of Taylor, Segalowitz and Gatbonton, and Haugen); and (3) the development and maintenance of language diversity in society (as represented by the papers of Tucker, and Fishman, Cooper, and Rosenbaum). The task of summarizing these reports is on the one hand made easy by their natural cohesiveness and on the other hand difficult by their diversity. I have chosen to organize this review around these three themes in order to facilitate integration of the contributions and in order to better point out their implications.

BILINGUALISM AND THE INDIVIDUAL

The question of whether the bilingual is cognitively different from the monolingual has been an issue of long-standing interest in bilingualism. A systematic investigation of it was first reported by Ronjat (1913) and later by Leopold (1949).

147

As Ben-Zeev points out in her chapter, interest in the topic was rekindled by Peal and Lambert (1962) with the publication of their now famous paper on intelligence and bilingualism.

The work of Sandra Ben-Zeev reflects an even more recent wave of renewed interest in this issue (see, for example, Balkan, 1970; Ianco-Worrall, 1972; Cummins & Gulutsan, 1974; and Bain, 1974). Ben-Zeev's contribution to this topic is particularly significant for a number of reasons. First of all, she has offered a well-argued and detailed theory of how and why bilinguals differ cognitively from monolinguals. This level of theorizing, albeit at times speculative, has been lacking for the most part until now. Secondly, she has been able to use this theoretical framework to integrate a variety of research findings more tightly than has previously been possible. And thirdly, from a more methodological point of view, her use of a replication study which manipulated some key variables while holding others constant is most commendable and generally desirable.

Ben-Zeev has suggested that "the benefits which accrue to the individual as a result of processes which arise to resist interlingual interference" will disappear to the extent that the two languages converge linguistically or to the extent that it is not important to the individuals to maintain their sociolinguistic distinctiveness for social psychological reasons. It can be asked, however, whether or not the effect of bilingualism as outlined by Ben-Zeev will also depend upon the individual's degree of bilingualism. Cummins (1976) has argued that the positive cognitive effects which have been reported by others (such as Peal and Lambert, 1962) are associated with the degree of relative balance of the two languages. Cummins presents data which suggests that non-balanced bilinguals, i.e., bilinguals who are native-like in only one of their languages, may in fact, experience negative cognitive effects. Cummins' argument is cogent indeed since most research on this topic has used balanced bilinguals as subjects; although the research of Scott, as reported by Lambert in Chapter 2, and of Genesee, Lambert, and Tucker (1976) was carried out with non-balanced bilinguals and still found evidence of positive outcomes. By way of answering my own question, it may be that whether or not non-balanced bilinguals benefit from their bilingualism will depend upon the reason for their lack of balance — individuals who have been unable to achieve equal proficiency in both languages despite considerable effort may still demonstrate cognitive benefits, whereas individuals who have failed to achieve balance because of a lack of effort to master the second language, owing perhaps to its low social value or utility, may not experience any benefits. Research would be required to test this hypothesis.

In a somewhat related vein, do individuals who become bilingual after the first language is well established experience
positive cognitive side effects and if so which ones? Most research on the cognitive effects of bilinguals has studied infant bilinguals, i.e., bilinguals who acquired their two languages concurrently. Individuals who learn their second language after their first language may experience less acute interlingual interference since they have already acquired and
consolidated one set of linguistic rules. Under these circumstances, the influence of bilingualism may be more superficial
with no significant effects on more profound cognitive processes. The converse argument could be made, however — when one
linguistic system has already been acquired and becomes dominant, then acquisition of a second language will produce greater interference as the individual must suppress the dominating
tendencies of the first-acquired language. This possibility
could be tested by studying children who have participated in
immersion-type second language programs where they are taught
exclusively via a second language during the primary grades
(c.f., Lambert & Tucker, 1972). A study by Genesee, Hamers,
Lambert, Mononen, Seitz and Starck (1976), to be discussed in
more detail in conjunction with McCormack's chapter, offers
preliminary evidence indicating that age of second language acquisition must be considered in studies on the consequences of
bilingualism.

In the final section of her chapter, Ben-Zeev raises an
important point — that the effect of bilingualism on cognitive
development will not necessarily be a main effect but rather
it may interact with social variables, such as the dominance
relationship of the two languages, or the prestige value of
each language. Lambert has made a similar point in his distinction between additive and subtractive forms of bilingualism. This distinction, along with that of Cummins, between
balanced and non-balanced bilinguals, represents an interesting
development in bilingual research because it is a move away
from a dichotomous classification of bilinguals and monolinguals toward a more complex taxonomy which includes bilingual
subtypes along with the basic bilingual/monolingual distinction.
The use of these additional distinctions in research may lead
to a more complete and coherent picture of bilingualism and
its consequences.

There has been a general tendency for research on the cognitive consequences of bilingualism to be isolated from the
more general topic of individual differences in cognitive development. This may be due to historical reasons, that is by
virtue of the early studies by Ronjat and Leopold; or perhaps
the "bad publicity" that surrounded bilingualism before the
sixties created a defensive research atmosphere. In any event,
I would like to suggest that a broader perspective on bilin-

gualism and cognitive development be adopted, one that would
view bilingualism as a point along a continuum of language or
life experiences which influence cognitive development. In
other words, there may be types of monlingualism or even of
nonlanguage experiences which have the same cognitive consequences as being bilingual. For example, is the greater or
lesser use of code switching (Gumperz & Hymes, 1972) associated
with any of the same cognitive concomitants which differentiate
bilinguals from monolinguals? Or, conversely, what are the
consequences of a relatively "impoverished" language repertoire,
such as characterizes illiteracy, on cognitive development
(Khadem, 1976)? A search for and understanding of these other
types of experiences might help us to better understand what
it is about being or becoming bilingual that is influential in
cognitive development.

In his chapter on the interdependence-independence issue,
McCormack has revisited another of the long-standing issues in
bilingual research, namely the cognitive representation of the
bilingual's two languages. This particular line of research
stems from the compound-coordinate hypothesis originally proposed by Weinreich (1953) and subsequently tested by others
(Ervin & Osgood, 1954; Lambert, Havelka, & Crosby, 1958; Lambert & Rawlings, 1969). McCormack's review of recent research
on this topic along with his reinterpretation of previous studies strongly favors the interdependence or compound hypothesis,
which postulates a single memory store for the bilingual's two
languages, or, from a more general linguistic point of view, a
single set of significates representing the signifiers in both
languages (Taylor, 1976).

As well as treating bilinguals as a single group, it might
be valuable to consider subgroups within the larger bilingual
grouping. In fact, the original compound-coordinate distinction was intended to differentiate between two subgroups of bilinguals, those who had learned both languages in a common context, the compound type, and those who had learned their two
languages in different contexts, the coordinate type. More recently, the compound-coordinate distinction has come to represent an age of acquisition distinction rather than a context of
acquisition distinction. Accordingly, acquisition of both languages in infancy (early bilinguality) is expected to result
in a compounded bilingual system whereas nonsimultaneous acquisition of the two languages (late bilinguality) is expected
to result in a coordinated bilingual system. Some support for
this distinction has been offered by Lambert and Rawlings
(1969) and by Lambert (1969) using the more traditional verbal
learning techniques and by Genesee, Hamers, Lambert, Mononen,
Seitz, and Starck (1976) using neurophysiological techniques.
In this latter study, we examined three groups of adult bilinguals: one group, the "infant bilinguals," had learned both

languages from infancy; a second group, the "childhood bilinguals," had acquired skill in the second language at approximately five years of age; and a third group, the "adolescent
bilinguals," had become bilingual at the high school age level.
All were balanced bilinguals at the time of testing; the age
range was eighteen to twenty-six years. The subjects were required to listen to a series of French and English words, presented monaurally through headphones, and to press a reaction
time key to indicate whether each word was French or English.
While performing this task their left and right hemisphere activity was monitored and recorded via surface electrodes to
provide average electroencephalic response (AER) comparisons
of the activity of the two hemispheres when French and English
stimuli were presented.

The results indicated that when considered as a single
group, the bilinguals demonstrated the characteristic pattern
of cerebral involvement for language processing — the left
hemisphere AERs (latency to N_1 and latency to P_2) were significantly faster than those of the right hemisphere — for both
French and English words. When the subgroups were considered
separately, however, we found that this left hemisphere advantage in speed of responding was limited to the infant and
childhood bilinguals. The adolescent bilinguals demonstrated
a faster *right* hemisphere response to both French and English
words under the same conditions. Furthermore, the adolescent
bilinguals had faster overall cortical responses than did the
other two groups.

These findings led us to speculate that the adolescent bilingual subgroup were using a more gestalt-like, holistic, or
possibly melodic, strategy to categorize the stimulus words.
These types of strategies are more characteristic of right
hemisphere functioning than of left (Levy-Agresti & Sperry,
1968; Ornstein, 1972; King & Kimura, 1972). The other bilingual subgroups, on the other hand, may have been using a more
semantic, analytic strategy which would be based in the left
hemisphere (Levy-Agresti & Sperry, 1968; Ornstein, 1972) and
would also take longer, perhaps owing to complications arising
from associational networks during semantic processing (Norman,
1970). These results also suggested to us that the different
components of the adolescent bilinguals' language processing
system — such as phonetic, semantic, and syntactic subroutines —
might be more differentiated neurophysiologically than those of
the infant or childhood bilinguals.

This research raises the further possibility that the interdependence or independence of the bilinguals' languages may
occur at a functional as well as at a structural level and,
therefore, that different aspects of the bilinguals' linguistic
systems will be more or less separate or overlapping. For example, Kolers (1963), using a free association technique with

mixed language stimulus words, found that there was more overlap between the bilinguals' associations for stimulus items
with denotative meanings (such as "table," "lamb") than for
items with connotative meanings (such as "freedom," "justice").
This would suggest that the bilinguals' semantic systems overlap for signifiers with concrete or objective referents, but
are more separated for signifiers with abstract, nonphysical
referents. Swain (1972) has made a similar suggestion about
the representation of grammatical units so that the bilingual
may have a single "grammar pool" for rules which are essentially the same in both languages but distinctive pools for rules
which are unique to each language. Other features of the bilinguals' linguistic system may be similarly organized. And,
as was suggested previously, the bilingual may not be a total-
ly unique creature so that the representational systems which
the bilingual develops to manage his linguistic complexity may
also characterize the nonbilingual with respect to different
or analogous types of linguistic complexity.

Bi-lingualism is not the only characteristic of the bilingual; for he may also be bicultural, and it was this aspect
of the bilingual which formed the focus of much of the chapter
by Lambert. This topic has been surrounded by considerable
controversy over the years (for reviews of this research see,
Diebold, 1968; Lamy, 1974) with many theoreticians and researchers claiming that to be bilingual engenders feelings of
anomie (Lamy, 1974), marginality (Meisel, in Lamy, 1974), and
even schizophrenia (Christophersen, 1948). It has been argued
that in learning two languages the bilingual must also inter-
nalize two systems of "shared meanings or world views" (Lamy,
1974, p. 4) one from each of the ethnolinguistic groups involved. It is argued further that identity problems arise
either because these meaning systems are inherently irreconc-
cilable and, therefore, create a type of schizophrenia or else
they are reconcilable but yield a hybrid reality system which
is not completely similar to the systems of either of the
groups whose languages he speaks. In his paper, Lambert cites
a study (cf., Gardner & Lambert, 1972) on the ethnic identity
of people with a dual cultural heritage which demonstrates that
individuals may indeed react in different ways to bicultural
backgrounds. This study which was carried out in French-American communities in New England and Louisiana found evidence for
at least three types of reactions. There were subgroups of individuals who oriented themselves exclusively toward one of
their two ethnolinguistic reference groups and ignored the others; subgroups who tried not to think of themselves in ethnic
terms; and, interestingly, subgroups who identified positively
with both of their ethnolinguistic reference groups. Thus, to
talk about bilingualism as if it had unconditionally negative
or positive sociocultural consequences would be a gross over-

simplification of the issues. The opposing contentions concerning the positive and negative consequences of bilingualism
on personality development or identity formation may be equally valid but require qualifications which clearly define the
subgroup and sociocultural circumstances involved. Much valuable research needs to be carried out to investigate those circumstances in which individuals have difficulty adjusting to
their bicultural heritage.

In this respect, Lambert has suggested that the consequences of bilingualism may depend upon the dominance of the
bilingual's two languages. He differentiates between additive
and subtractive forms of bilingualism. Additive bilingualism
is characterized by the acquisition of two socially useful and
prestigious languages which are mutually viable. Subtractive
bilingualism, on the other hand, occurs when the acquisition
of one language threatens to replace or dominate the other language. This latter situation is most likely to happen with
members of ethnic minority groups such as Spanish Americans or
French Canadians for whom the acquisition of English very often results in the gradual loss of the native language. Subtractive bilingualism may also be accompanied by subtractive
biculturalism to the extent that the language and the culture
of the group are interwoven, and to the extent that the culture of the dominant language group threatens to replace or
dominate the culture of the nondominant language group. Taylor
is in basic agreement with this position; he contends that
"threats to ethnic identity, which arise from inequalities in
intergroup relations may alter the motivational balance for becoming bilingual."

It follows from this that the type of bilingual education
one would prescribe for members of minority groups would differ from that for members of the majority group. For children
from the majority group, education exclusively in a second language during all or part of their schooling is more likely to
lead to additive forms of bilingualism and biculturalism. Research which we have been conducting in Canada illustrates this
point. I am referring here to the St. Lambert French immersion
school experiment (Lambert & Tucker, 1972) and other similar
immersion programs in the Montreal area (Polich, 1974; Genesee,
Polich, & Stanley, 1976; Genesee, Sheiner, Tucker, & Lambert,
1976). In these experimental programs, children from the na-
tionally dominant English-Canadian group who are educated exclusively in French during the primary grades and subsequently
in French and English during the senior grades develop the same
linguistic, academic and cognitive competence as children who
are educated in the regular English schools. As Lambert notes
in his chapter, children in these programs have not demonstrated any difficulty in reconciling this "French immersion experience" with their essentially English-Canadian background.

There is no evidence at all that acquisition of a second language and interaction with members of the related ethnic group
under the immersion conditions in any way threatens these children's native language or culture. We have recent evidence
that even Anglophone children in *all* French schools, that is
schools where the majority of the pupils as well as all the
teachers are French-speaking, develop the same degree of identity with their native English-Canadian group as do children in
the regular English program (Genesee, 1974). Thus, we have
here examples of an additive form of bilingual/bicultural education for majority group children.

What was surprising to us about the Anglophone children
in the all French schools was a finding that by grade 3 they
did not seem to have developed any stronger sense of identity
with the French-Canadian group whose language they were learning than did children in the English schools. It may well be
that for the majority group child at least the cultural orientation of the home is more powerful than that of the school in
the development of an ethnic identity; the children in this
study were all from monolingual English homes. It would be
important to pursue this study by extending it to higher grade
levels and also by investigating the implications of these
findings for the participating children's second-language
learning especially in view of the reported saliency of integrative motives in second-language learning (Gardner & Lambert,
1972).

Because Anglo-American or Anglo-Canadian children can be
successfully educated in a second language does not necessarily mean that the most effective educational technique for non-
English-speaking children in America would be a second-language
approach using English. Such a situation might result in subtractive bilingualism for the reasons outlined earlier. On the
contrary, it might be advisable to adopt a native-language approach with non-English-speaking minority group children at
least during the primary grades, so that the children's native
language and culture can become firmly rooted. Subsequent exposure to the English language and its associate culture at
higher grade levels might then occur more easily and with more
positive consequences (Genesee, 1976). In other words, as
Lambert has suggested, by first of all nurturing and supporting the language and culture which are most likely to be neglected by the society, then later introduction of a second language and culture may be a more additive process.

In many of the Title VII projects in the United States
use of the child's native language in the primary grades is regarded as transitional and essentially remedial — conditions
which are not likely to engender positive bilingual experiences. In order to maximize the chances of additive bilingualism, it would be important to reverse this attitude. This

might be achieved by ensuring that the transition to English in bilingual programs would not bring about the complete replacement of the child's native language as a means of communication in the school. This could be avoided easily by maintaining some course instruction in the native language, mathematics or science, for example. Careful and systematic evaluation of specially selected Title VII bilingual schools would provide a test of some of the hypotheses previously discussed. Such an evaluation should include measures of social psychological development as well as of linguistic, academic, and cognitive development since the notion of additive bilingualism contends that successful academic learning will take place only if we take care of the child's social psychological needs, particularly as they relate to his ethnic identity.

I do not wish to appear to be proselitizing for education in the vernacular for minority group children, but rather I wish to argue for alternative forms of education. Since groups with dual or multiple cultural backgrounds react to their heritage differently (cf., Gardner & Lambert, 1972) it may be appropriate to provide them with alternative kinds of school experiences. Just as the traditional forms of education in our English schools may not be uniformly effective for all children, education in a non-English, vernacular language may not be uniformly effective for all non-English-speaking minority group children. It is for this reason that the work of Lambert, Taylor, and others who are similarly interested in the psychosocial consequences of bilingualism is important. By leading us to a greater recognition and understanding of some of the different types of bilingualism and biculturalism and their etiology, this type of research may allow us to transform the subtractive forms into more additive forms.

BILINGUAL COMMUNITIES

The decision to include the chapters by Taylor, Haugen, and Segalowitz and Gatbonton in a separate section on bilingual communities is somewhat arbitrary since some of the ideas presented in these papers could easily have been discussed in the preceding section. Conversely, some aspects of Lambert's paper from the preceding section are clearly relevant to the current discussion. Nevertheless, I think that taken together in a separate section these papers provide an interesting and relatively new perspective on bilingualism, one that focuses on social factors which affect the structure of languages in contact, language use, and even second-language learning in bilingual communities.

In an interesting series of studies on the nonfluent bilingual, Segalowitz and Gatbonton demonstrated that it is pos-

sible to describe the linguistic performance of a population
of second-language users including all members of the population regardless of their second-language proficiency. Furthermore, the technique they present relates pattern of linguistic
variation to level of proficiency in a systematic way by describing second-language variation as a series of approxima-
tions to the linguistic form used by native speakers of the
language. They found that level of development as determined
by this type of linguistic analysis correlated .80 or better
with proficiency rankings assigned by native speakers. This
is indeed a very useful technique since it provides a comprehensive linguistic analysis of second-language skills, which
cannot be achieved easily using other techniques, and at the
same time relates this to proficiency level as judged by native speakers of the language.

The work presented by Haugen suggests that the nonfluent
bilingual in a bilingual community may never be able to completely match the native language users' language since in a
bilingual community there are a variety of communication demands made on even the fluent bilingual which cause his languages to "deviate" from their respective standard forms as
spoken by monolingual native speakers. Haugen does not, however, view these variations from standard form as "deviations."
Rather, he contends that they represent interlinguistic borrowings which are a natural and utilitarian result of languages
in contact. Haugen enumerates a number of rules which describe
the patterns of borrowings that are most likely to occur when
two languages are in contact. Thus, according to Haugen, the
variations which come to characterize the bilinguals' languages
might be considered as communicative norms which reflect the
particular communication patterns of bilinguals in a bilingual community.

By integrating the work of Segalowitz and Gatbonton and
Haugen it might be possible to determine which of the nonfluent bilinguals' second-language variations meet the communicative demands of his community and which do not. The acquisition and possible fossilization of communicatively nonfunc-
tional or dysfunctional second-language variations may lead to
frustrating and negative experiences with native speakers of
the language which could, in turn, have negative effects on
the second-language learner's motivation to continue learning
the language. For similar reasons, it might be important to
investigate native speakers' attitudinal reactions to second-
language users' linguistic variations. Native speakers of the
language might be prepared to tolerate certain variants but
not others. A second-language speaker who exceeds the tolerance level of the native-language community might meet with
rejection. Finally, if the standard or form of the second-
language learner's second language does not meet his own ex-

pectations and requirements, disillusionment could set in.
Segalowitz and Gatbonton's study on the use of the colloquial
form of the second language with native speakers illustrates
this point clearly.

It is important in bilingual communities where second-
language speakers are likely to use the second language with
native speakers that they acquire necessary and sufficient communication skills, as Segalowitz and Gatbonton point out.
Failure to do so could result in negative social interactions
with native speakers leading to an avoidance of similar interactions in the future and, perhaps, even to a loss of motivation to pursue second-language learning. Thus, more research
needs to be carried out to determine the nature and limits of
variation which a language community will accept from second-
language speakers. A number of interesting side issues arise;
for example, are the limits of linguistic variation a function
of the second-language user's group membership — for example,
will French Canadians accept the same type and amounts of linguistic variation in French when spoken as a second language
by English Canadians and Americans?

Language use in bilingual communities has also become a
topic of recent research interest. Taylor notes that bilinguals may use their language to express cooperation or conflict — bilinguals who accommodate their language to correspond to their interlocuters' native language are likely to be
judged favorably and are also likely to meet with a corresponding accommodative response from the interlocuter; on the other
hand, bilinguals who choose to use their own native language
with an interlocuter who speaks another native language are
likely to be judged less favorably and to be met with a similar nonaccommodative response by their interlocuter (see also
Giles, 1973). Choice of language is perhaps but the most simple accommodative language response. Other, more subtle accommodative responses, such as the use of "tu" versus "vous"
in French, may be less easily learned by second-language learners but nevertheless may have significant social consequences.
Thus, bilinguals who do not know the appropriate accommodative
response in certain social exchanges but nevertheless would
like to indicate accommodation may be judged unjustifiably
negatively by their interlocuters. As the emphasis in North
American schools moves away from the teaching of foreign or
second languages toward developing intercultural communication
skills, more and more emphasis will necessarily rest on teaching the sociocultural rules of second-language use (Genesee,
1976). These types of language rules are not easily found in
textbooks and cannot easily be taught the way grammatical rules
can be taught. They are, nonetheless, important if successful
cross-cultural communication is to be effected.

Gatbonton (1975) reports that the way a person speaks a

second language can influence the political attitudes which are attributed to him by others within his own group. Persons with nativelike or near nativelike pronunciation in the second language were judged to hold attitudes favorable toward native speakers of the language, whereas persons with a heavily accented second language were judged to hold attitudes strongly in favor of the home group. This study illustrates another way in which languages in bilingual communities can be used as social tools. By shifting their way of speaking with either their home group or with the second-language group, second-language speakers can indicate their degree of group affiliation. This presupposes that the second-language speaker has the capacity to shift registers and that members of the second-language group associate the same kinds of attitudes with level of second-language proficiency as do members of the home group.

These findings are interesting for two additional reasons. First of all, as Segalowitz and Gatbonton note, they indicate that language groups may hold common perceptions or beliefs about the relationship between second-language proficiency and attitudes. Second, they suggest that second-language learning patterns may be affected by social pressures within the home group. Thus, insofar as attributions of in-group orientation may depend upon one's skill in the second language and insofar as some communities may value in-group membership to varying degrees, there may be more or less incentive in some communities to develop nativelike competence in the language. These hypotheses could be tested using the second-language classroom as a pseudo-community — that is, are there norms in second-language classrooms which are based on the value of in-group membership and which mitigate against or encourage acquisition of nativelike competence? This would be important to determine since such norms could influence the level of competence that could be expected in the second-language classroom regardless of curriculum objectives and procedures.

In summary, the research reported by Haugen, Taylor, and Segalowitz and Gatbonton provide some very exciting new insights about bilingualism. We have read evidence which suggests that there are communicative and social norms in bilingual communities that influence the kind of language we learn and use. It has been suggested further that the ways in which we speak our second language or the very fact of our speaking a second language may influence the way we are seen and reacted to by members of our home group and by members of the second-language group. As in a monolingual setting, language in a bilingual community becomes an important and powerful social tool expressing interpersonal and intergroup intentions and motivations. The implications which I have drawn from these studies for second-language learning, intergroup communication and person perception are but a few of the more obvious ones.

It is evident that this approach to studying bilingualism will
prove very valuable indeed.

LANGUAGE DIVERSITY IN SOCIETY

The final two chapters, by Fishman, Cooper, and Rosenbaum
and by Tucker, represent an additional dimension to the study
of bilingualism, namely, the development and maintenance of
language diversity in society. Fishman *et al.*'s research on
English Around the World illustrates a phenomenon which is evident to even the most casual traveler, that is, the increasing
prevalence of English as a world language. Fishman and his
colleagues found that chief among the variables determining
the prevalence of English in various spheres of a country's activities were: (1) former anglophone colonial status; (2) pre-
existing linguistic diversity; (3) religious composition; and
(4) educational and economic development. Among the many interesting findings that emerged from this extensive study were
two which particularly caught my attention. One pertains to
the suggestion that the concept of an instrumental motivation
for second-language learning may have an analog at the national level. Thus, Fishman found that exports predicted the prevalence of the English language in a country better than did
imports. This places the economically developed Anglophone
countries of the world in a powerful position to influence the
maintenance of national languages. Failure of the developed
countries to do international business in national languages
will enhance the necessity for the developing countries to anglicize that sphere of their society. The second finding
which caught my attention was that developing nations find it
more difficult than other nations to provide secondary school
education through local, vernacular languages. This point is
well illustrated by many of the Arab countries which until recently have provided virtually all post-elementary education
in a non-Arabic language, French or English. Consequently,
with a move toward universal education, developing countries
may be required to anglicize even further.

Tucker has also noted that the developing countries have
a demonstrated need for foreign-language proficiency, particularly in the world languages, and that this need is continuing
to grow presumably as a result of some of the factors which
Fishman has delineated. Paradoxically, however, Tucker also
notes that there is a growing trend toward vernacularization,
at least insofar as education is concerned, in some of these
same countries. To this end, some developing countries are
cutting back on the time devoted to teaching foreign languages
in school and are in the process of vernacularizing their
school systems. In order to reconcile these two countervail-

ing tendencies, one toward world languages and one toward vernacular languages, Tucker suggests that it will be increasingly necessary to provide the most effective second-language programs possible so that proficiency in the world languages,
such as English, can be achieved at no expense to the maintenance and development of vernacular languages. In view of
Fishman's finding that the poorer developing countries may
have difficulty providing education, and especially secondary
education, in the vernacular, then increased responsibility
will fall to the developing countries to assist in the creation of instructional materials and curricula in a variety of
"non-world" languages. This in turn can only happen if the
developing countries express more appreciation and sensitivity
to other languages and cultures.

While Tucker is somewhat optimistic that a healthy balance between second-language learning and vernacularization
can be and is being achieved in the developing nations, he is
less than optimistic about the situation back home, in North
America. There is movement afoot in North America to vernacu-
larize education for non-English-speaking children or for children who do not speak standard white English. It is hoped
that education in the vernacular will also give these children
greater access to the English educational system. Thus, the
Bilingual Education Act of 1967, in the United States, has provided the legislative impetus to educate children in their
native language, at least during the primary grades. Similar
programs on a much smaller scale and on a less official basis
have been started in Canada as well (see Purbhoo & Shapson,
1975; and Durwood, Moody, & Ellis, 1973).

As both Tucker and Taylor point out we have the pedagogic-
al expertise to train students in second languages; this is no
longer a problem. Tucker's pessimism arises from the failure
of the majority group to demonstrate a readiness to receive
the product of these bilingual programs. Bilingualism is often seen as a temporary, transitional state on the way to a
monolingual English state. Taylor was similarly concerned
about the attitudes of the dominant cultural group toward members of other language groups. Accordingly, he suggested that,
contrary to traditional social psychological theories of attitude change, it may be possible to alter attitudes by altering
behavior (Bem, 1970), which in the case of a nation can be effected through legislation. Regardless of how change occurs,
most would probably agree that acceptance of bilingualism
among Middle Americans will require a redefinition of national
identities and value systems to include linguistic and cultural diversity for themselves as well as for minority groups.
While sharing some of Tucker's pessimism, I would like to add,
along with Lambert, that there are optimistic signs, albeit
faint, which reflect a change in the majority group's attitude

toward bilingualism. Along with those examples which Lambert
has listed, I would include the second-language immersion programs for Anglo-American children which have recently been developed in the United States; these include the Culver City
and Redwood City Spanish Immersion Projects in California
(Cohen, 1974; Cohen, Fathman, & Merino, 1976) and a new French
Immersion Project in Plattsburgh, New York (W. Derrick, personal communication). These innovations represent small but
noteworthy changes in cultural attitudes; their ultimate significance will not be known for some time, however. In any
event, the viability of bilingualism and of bilingual education in the United States and in Canada, may well be in the
hands of the dominant Anglophone groups.

In conclusion, it should have become evident to the reader that the patterns of growth in bilingual research are both
horizontal and vertical. The entire base of bilingual research
has been broadened and subdivided; we have moved away from a
simple same-different conceptualization of the bilingual-monolingual distinction to a more complex conceptualization which
sees distinctions within the bilingual population itself and
which hopefully will soon begin to integrate bilingual research
with research on individual differences in development. On
top of this, we are adding new dimensions of inquiry, dimensions which reflect social psychological, sociolinguistic, and
educational theories.

REFERENCES

Bain, B.C. Bilingualism and cognition: Towards a general
    theory. In S. Carey (Ed.), *Bilingualism, biculturalism
    and education*. Proceedings from the conference at College
    Universitaire Saint-Jean, The University of Alberta,
    1974.
Balkan, L. *Les effets du bilinguisme francais-anglais sur
    les aptitudes intellectuelles*. Bruxelles: Aimav, 1970.
Bem, D.J. *Beliefs, attitudes and human affairs*. Belmont,
    Calif." Wadsworth, 1970.
Ben-Zeev, S. The influence of bilingualism on cognitive
    development and cognitive strategy. Ph.D. dissertation.
    Department of Human Development, University of Chicago,
    1972.
Ben-Zeev, S. The effect of Spanish-English bilingualism in
    children from less privileged neighborhoods on cognitive
    development and cognitive strategy. Bilingual Education
    Service, Arlington Heights, Illinois, 1975.
Christophersen, P. *Bilingualism*. London: Methuen, 1948.
Cohen, A. The Culver City Spanish immersion program: The
    first two years. *The Modern Language Journal*, 1974, *58*,

95-103.

Cohen, A., Fathman, A., & Merino, B. The Redwood City Bilingual Education Project, 1971-1974: Spanish and English proficiency, mathematics and language use over time. *Working Papers in Bilingualism*, 1976, No. 8, 1-29.

Cummins, J. Cognitive factors associated with the attainment of intermediate levels of bilingual skills. Mimeo, Center for Study of Mental Retardation, University of Alberta, Edmonton, 1976.

Cummins, J., & Gulutsan, M. Symbolic coding in bilinguals. In S. Carey (Ed.), *Bilingualism, biculturalism and education*. Proceedings from the conference at College Universitaire Saint-Jean, The University of Alberta, 1974.

Diebold, A.R. The consequences of early bilingualism on cognitive development and personality formation. In Norbeck, Price-Williams & McCord (Eds.), *The study of personality: An interdisciplinary appraisal*. New York: Holt, Rinehart & Winston, 1968.

Durwood, M.L., Moody, J.L., & Ellis, E.N. Evaluation of the Punjabi-English class at Moberly Primary Annex for the 1972-73 school year. Report from the Board of School Trustees, Department of Planning and Evaluation, Vancouver, B.C., 1973, No. 73-20.

Ervin, S.M., & Osgood, C.E. Second language learning and bilingualism. *Journal of Abnormal and Social Psychology*. Suppl., 1954, *49*, 139-146.

Gardner, R., & Lambert, W.E. *Attitudes and motivation in second-language learning*. Rowley, Mass.: Newbury House, 1972.

Gatbonton, E. Systematic variations in second-language speech: a sociolinguistic study. Unpublished Ph.D. dissertation, Department of Linguistics, McGill University, 1975.

Genesee, F. Bilingual education: social psychological consequences. Unpublished Ph.D. thesis, Department of Psychology, McGill University, 1974.

Genesee, F.H. Some Canadian experiments in developing intercultural communication. Paper presented at the Central States Conference on the Teaching of Foreign Languages, Detroit, April, 1976.

Genesee, F.H., Hamers, J., Lambert, W.E., Mononen, L., Seitz, M., & Starck, R. A study of cerebral dominance in bilinguals. Paper presented at the International Neuropsychology Society Conference, Toronto, Canada, February, 1976.

Genesee, F., Polich, E., & Stanley, M. An experimental French immersion program at the secondary school level — 1969 to 1974. In press, *The Canadian Modern Language*

Review, 1976.

Genesee, F., Sheiner, E., Tucker, G.R., & Lambert, W.E. An experiment in trilingual education. *The Canadian Modern Language Review,* 1976, *32,* 115-128.

Genesee, F., Tucker, G.R., & Lambert, W.E. Communication skills of bilingual children. *Child Development,* 1975, *46,* 1010-1014.

Giles, H. Accent mobility: model and some data. *Anthropological Linguistics,* 1973, *15,* 87-105.

Gumperz, J.J., & Hymes, D. *Directions in sociolinguistics.* New York: Holt, Rinehart & Winston, 1972.

Ianco-Worrall, A.D. Bilingualism and cognitive development. *Child Development,* 1972, *43,* 1390-1400.

Khadem, F. The development of cerebral laterality in illiterate and literate children and adults — a preliminary study. In preparation, Psychology Department, McGill University, 1976.

King, F.L., & Kimura, D. Left ear superiority in dichotic perception of vocal nonverbal sounds. *Canadian Journal of Psychology,* 1972, *26,* 111-116.

Kolers, P.A. Interlingual word associations. *Journal of Verbal Learning and Verbal Behavior,* 1963, *2,* 291-300.

Lambert, W.E. Psychological studies of interdependencies of the bilingual's two languages. In J. Purvel (Ed.), *Substance and structure of language.* Los Angeles: University of California Press, 1969. Pp. 99-126.

Lambert, W.E., Havelka, J., & Crosby, C. The influence of language acquisition contexts on bilingualism. *Journal of Abnormal and Social Psychology,* 1958, *56,* 239-244.

Lambert, W.E., & Rawlings, C. Bilingual processing of mixed language associative networks. *Journal of Verbal Learning and Verbal Behavior,* 1969, *8,* 604-609.

Lambert, W.E., & Tucker, G.R. *The bilingual education of children: The St. Lambert Experiment.* Rowley, Mass.: Newbury House, 1972.

Lamy, P. The impact of bilingualism upon ethnolinguistic identity. Paper presented at the VIIIth World Congress of Sociology, Toronto, Canada, August, 1974.

Leopold, W.F. *Speech development of a bilingual child* (Vol. 3). Evanston: Northwestern University Press, 1949.

Levy-Agresti, J., & Sperry, R.W. Differential perceptual capacities in major and minor hemispheres. *Proceedings of the National Academy of Sciences,* 1968, *61,* 115.

Macnamara, J. *Bilingualism and primary education.* Edinburgh: University Press, 1966.

Norman, D.A. (Ed.) *Models of human memory.* New York: Academic Press, 1970.

Ornstein, R.E. *The psychology of consciousness*. San Francisco: W.H. Freeman & Co., 1972.

Peal, E., & Lambert, W.E.   The relation of bilingualism to intelligence. *Psychological Monographs, 76*, 1962.

Polich, E.   Report on the Evaluation of the Lower Elementary French Immersion Programme through Grade III, 1971-1973. Curriculum Department, the Protestant School Board of Greater Montreal, 1974.

Purbhoo, M., & Shapson, S.   Transition from Italian. Report from the Board of Education for the City of Toronto, 1975, No. 133.

Ronjat, J.   *Le developpement du langage observe chez un enfant bilingue*. Paris: Champion, 1913.

Swain, M.   Bilingualism as a first language. Ph.D. thesis, Department of Psychology, University of California, Irvine, 1972.

Taylor, I.   *Introduction to psycholinguistics*. New York: Holt, Rinehart & Winston, 1976.

Weinreich, U.   *Languages in contact*. New York: Publications of Linguistic Circle, 1953.

Index